MW00605056

For the Andrews clan,
a family whose great joy, love, and generosity of spirit
have continued through the generations

FIONA SOLTES

Virtuous SERVANT

Sarah Sheppard Andrews

Christian Missionary to Japan

Providence House Publishers
WWW.PROVIDENCEHOUSE.COM
FRANKLIN, TENNESSEE

Printed in the United States of America

13   12   11   10   09   1   2   3   4   5

Library of Congress Control Number: 2008942214

ISBN: 978-1-57736-416-0

Cover design by LeAnna Massingille
Page design by LeAnna Massingille, Joey McNair, and Melissa Istre

Scripture quotations marked KJV are taken from the Holy Bible, King James Version, Cambridge, 1796.

PROVIDENCE HOUSE PUBLISHERS
238 Seaboard Lane • Franklin, Tennessee 37067
www.providencehouse.com
800-321-5692

CONTENTS

Virtue in itself is not enough; there must also be the power to translate it into action.

—Aristotle

Virtue is not knowing but doing.

—Japanese proverb

The path of a good woman is indeed strewn with flowers; but they rise behind her steps, not before them.

—John Ruskin

FOREWORD

The life of Sarah Sheppard Andrews is a beacon to all who strive to make their lives sublime by good works, leaving behind a legacy of goodwill. Seriously ill, facing starvation, separated from friends, surrounded by the enemy, isolated, but never alone, she refused to give up. Hers was a Christian life fulfilled.

The effort to preserve my aunt's story began in 1984, some twenty years after her death. Sumitomo Corporation of Japan located an important industrial plant in Dickson, Tennessee, with several new Japanese managers. I, as chairman of the Dickson County Industrial Board, became acquainted with Koichiro "Tom" Tamura, senior vice president and general manager. I related the story of Sarah's journey, and it stirred in him an interest to visit her hometown and learn more when he returned to Japan. His visit to Shizuoka, as well as interviews with older friends and second-generation residents, made a deep impression on him of her many good works and the profound respect that remains for her still. He was especially moved by her Christian influence and the spirit of goodwill she bestowed on those who knew her.

Since then, much work has been done to collect information on her life and times. Both my wife, Roberta Neblett Andrews, and sister, Bettie Andrews Lundy, have shared it with ladies' group meetings and church audiences, but it is our hope that her story can travel beyond those presentations. It is our hope that some will read of her life and be inspired to follow in her courageous footsteps. Her influence lives on.

We wish to express our appreciation to the author, Fiona Soltes, for her personal interest and skill, and to extend our good wishes to the future Sarahs out there. May you pick up her torch.

Dan Beasley Andrews, nephew
Dickson, Tennessee

PREFACE AND ACKNOWLEDGMENTS

We would not know the details of the life of Sarah Sheppard Andrews had she not written of them herself; her personal letters to family and friends were rich with description, offering an inside look at her remarkable adventures. Sarah's relatives in particular are fortunate that so many of these letters still exist, including those to her sister Myrtle and mother, Ada, and to Elizabeth McCaleb and husband, J. M. McCaleb, who were Sarah's inspiration for going to Japan.

Without those letters and without the work of journalists writing for *Word and Work* and *Gospel Advocate*, *Virtuous Servant: Sarah Sheppard Andrews, Christian Missionary to Japan* would not exist—Sarah Andrews's story would be almost impossible to tell. But because these articles were written by various persons of so long ago, as were Sarah's letters, the rules of the English language have changed. Therefore, Providence House Publishers has taken liberty to make the book more consistent throughout by editing quoted material if needed, making corrections only to capitalization and punctuation.

The book would have also been impossible without the recollections of family members who so fondly remember Sarah. As young children who were her nieces and nephews, they did not understand her fascinating dedication to an unknown people in a faraway world until they were much, much older. Aunt Sarah was always of good humor and fun, but to them, she was the bizarre aunt who lived overseas and would not stay home to take care of herself. Those nieces and nephews, such as Dan Andrews and Bettie Lundy, keep the warm spirit of Sarah Andrews alive here on earth today.

Bettie Lundy, Dan Andrews, and his wife, Roberta, proved to be very resourceful and were monumental in collecting stories and pictures. Lundy credits Brother Harry Robert Fox Jr. for photos of Sarah, for he graciously pulled many from his scrapbook and just handed them over without hesitation for the project. He was also a good storyteller.

The staff at Providence House who helped with the concept, the editing, and the design must also be commended. Even though Sarah was extremely modest and humble and would have discouraged any publicity of her good works, she would have been very pleased.

CHAPTER ONE

Lessons in Geography

Lift up your eyes, and look on the fields;
for they are white already to harvest.

JOHN 4:35

Some have ideas; some have dreams. Sarah Andrews had something different altogether: a heart of conviction plus a one-way ticket for making it reality.

She was only twenty-three when she set sail for Japan, not yet knowing that the days ahead would bring bombings, house arrest, near starvation, torment, persecution, loneliness, and illness. All she knew was that she had to go.

It was 1915.

Back then, women were still a few years shy of being able to vote. World War I had begun the year before, and in Cleveland, Ohio, a

3

curious new contraption aided those still getting used to the idea of automobiles: the world's first red and green traffic lights.

Sarah was an adventure waiting to happen. Strengthened with resolve, studied up for her journey, and ready to see what her Lord had in store, she stepped onto the boat.

The truth is, Sarah's voyage began long before that trip off the West Coast. It began back in tiny Dickson, Tennessee, on a day that could have been a Sunday like any other. Only it wasn't, thanks to a visit from Brother J. M. McCaleb, a seasoned missionary who came to tell the Walnut Street Church of Christ congregation about his various ventures across the globe. History is fuzzy on the exact date of the encounter, but this much is certain: young Sarah was all ears.

No doubt the church service had been a rousing one. McCaleb, author of numerous books about his experiences abroad, was known to show curious congregants back in the States a map representing "the world and the entire human race."[1] He spoke passionately of the great commission in the Bible to "Go ye into all the world, and preach the gospel to every creature" (Mark 16:15), but at the same time, said a lesson in geography was essential for that to happen.

From the pulpit, McCaleb would motion to his great map, one in which the word "heathen" was written across an area holding "a little more than half of the world's population, or about 800 million." Other marks showed "Mohammedanism," later to be known as Islam; the Greek Church; the Roman Catholics; and Protestantism. "Now this is not a very pleasing picture, but we have to deal with things as they are, not as we would have them be," he told a crowd gathered in Nashville, Tennessee, in 1910. "There must be an obligation on the part of those who have the light to take it to those who have not."[2]

When speaking of Japan in particular, McCaleb noted that missions work there had only taken place for about fifty years, compared to two hundred in India and one hundred in China.[3]

He would go through great detail about the idols and various gods that were revered in the land so far away, and tell of odd customs, such as the scattering of cooked beans around houses to drive out evil spirits.[4]

Japan and her people could have seemed as far away as the moon, but McCaleb had a way of driving his point home. "Were it not that we have been enlightened somewhat by the light that has come from above," he said, "we today would be doing exactly the same things that the Japanese people are doing across the sea."[5]

What of the American superstition, he asked, of planting potatoes "on the light of the moon" so they would all go to vine? What of the practice of carrying an Irish potato in the pocket to ward off rheumatism, or of tacking up horseshoes for good luck?[6]

And as for the worship of idols, he asked—showing the various objects he had brought back from his journeys—what of the images of saints like Thomas, Peter, Paul, Bartholomew, Andrew, Mary, and Jesus himself easily found in American churches?

"We do not go to the full extent that they do," he continued, "but nevertheless, we have enough respect for the dead, enough superstition and idolatry, to identify us very closely with our neighbors across the sea; and instead of these things being an evidence that these people are separated from the rest of the race, they rather go to show that we are all very much alike, and to serve rather as so many links connecting the whole human race together as one."[7]

McCaleb would give many such talks, pleading for workers to join in the harvest. At his 1910 Nashville talk, he claimed that there was only one missionary for every 61,000 people in Japan. Beyond that, in the city of Tokyo alone, there were 150,000 shrines and temples competing for the attention of the spiritually minded;[8] it wasn't hard to see how great the need actually was.

"Seventy-five percent of the believers in Japan have been won during the last ten years," McCaleb said.[9] But what of the next ten? Were the fields really that ripe for the harvest? Sarah would make herself ready to find out.

CHAPTER TWO

For Such a Time as This

Train up a child in the way he should go:
and when he is old, he will not depart from it.

PROVERBS 22:6

Sarah Andrews wasn't the first missionary to go to Japan. She wasn't even the first single woman. And yet, there is something unique to her journey, something that remains as inspirational and challenging today as it was all those years ago.

Sarah, according to those who knew her, was single-minded in focus. Once she made up her mind to go to Japan—after she approached J. M. McCaleb in that service in Dickson and vowed that she, too, would spread the Gospel overseas—she spent the following years learning all she might need to know. And once she actually arrived, she committed to stay no matter what—even if the simple

7

fact that the Good News she attempted to share wasn't always seen as good and no church back home consistently supported her financially. By the time she died in 1961, however (after only four trips back home to America), she was revered, respected, and known as one who preached through actions rather than words. So great was her impact that a monument was erected in her honor, and even twenty years after her death, one hundred people attended a memorial service held in her honor.[1]

So what was it about her that was so special? What was it that gave her the measure of steadfastness that others could barely fathom? Where did she gather the strength to sleep soundly even when chaos surrounded her? The answer lies in her simple faith, one that was formed and cultivated in Tennessee and in full bloom by the time it reached foreign shores.

Sarah Sheppard Andrews was born on November 26, 1892, in that same small town in Tennessee where she first encountered McCaleb, about forty miles from Nashville. That same year, Harper's *New Monthly Magazine* satirically commented on Thomas Edison's recent claims of being able to send someone across the country by electric rail at the rate of one hundred miles per hour, explained the manufacturing of ice (which not long before had been imported from the mountains rather than man-made), and pondered the shape of education in the newer states of the West.[2]

There was also great anticipation for the soon-to-be-open 1893 World's Columbian Exposition in Chicago, an event that would bring in South Sea Islanders, Eskimos, Turks, and others out of curiosity as well as give the world its first Ferris wheel; the United States, its Pledge of Allegiance; and Chicago, the first Midway.[3]

Yes, people traveled then, especially for such a curiosity. On one day alone, more than 751,000 people visited the Chicago fair, anxious to see just how the Americans could best Paris's Exposition Universelle in 1889, when the French had startled the world with the unveiling of the Eiffel Tower.[4]

It was a time of great promise, of new inventions and breaking down borders. The turn of the century found the United States the most affluent in the world, and more and more money was going toward vacations and leisure. Within the United States, there was a steam railroad network of some 200,000 miles and 14,000 more on electric. A train could now take a traveler the same distance in six days that a covered wagon had previously gone in six months. Some also traveled overseas by steamship, both the wealthy looking for adventure and the missionaries hoping to find converts.

McCaleb had been stationed in Japan since 1892, when he joined a band of believers sent to start a mission station with Christian pioneer Wilson Kendrick Azbill.[5] Though McCaleb had a great impact on Sarah's decision to do the same, he wasn't her only link to the then-termed "Orient." Missionary Kate Johnson was a friend of Sarah's mother who stayed with the Andrews family when returning to the States.[6]

It's no surprise that Sarah and her siblings would be aware of missions, given the strong faith of their parents. Will and Adele Andrews had come to Dickson via Hurricane Mills, a village less than twenty miles away. Once there, it didn't take long for them to discover that there was no Church of Christ in the area. So they gathered up a few like-minded folks and started one. According to the records of Walnut Street Church of Christ, Adele (known as Ada) was joined by several other women in securing a space above the

Dickson Bank and Trust Company,[7] and her husband Will agreed to pay the rent for the first few months.[8]

The first meeting at the facility was in May 1891. By the next year, the small congregation was preparing to build its own house of worship, and the Andrews family was preparing for an expansion, too. Sarah would be the fourth of nine children, and by the time she was fourteen, would be baptized in the same little church. Her siblings were Rob, Myrtle, Pete, Kate, Douglas, Bess, Nell, and Mark, but Douglas (just more than two years her junior) was Sarah's closest friend among the close-knit family. Ada instilled in them not only a devotion to service, but also a love for God.

Those who knew Ada knew that she had long dreamed of being a missionary herself; founding the congregation in Dickson, then, was somewhat of opportunity to do so on familiar soil. Family members recall that no matter where the Andrews family lived in its various homes around Dickson, they were always close enough to hear the church bells chime.

But religion wasn't the only emphasis of the burgeoning Andrews family. Education was also near the top of the list. In the early 1900s, only 4 percent of people age eighteen or older had completed high school,[9] but that made no difference to the Andrews clan. Ada credited her parents for instilling in her the importance of schooling, having both been well-educated themselves.[10] While in Hurricane Mills, her father worked for G. W. Hillman's mills, which processed flour, corn, and wool.

Dickson, however, offered the children new opportunities. Dickson Normal College had been established in 1885, and in 1919, it became the site of the county's first four-year high school.[11] Young Sarah, like her siblings, was offered solid schooling, and she took full advantage of everything available in case it could be of use to her in the future. In addition to public speaking and art, she studied first aid, home economics, and even the teaching of kindergarten. Her education continued at West Tennessee Normal School in Memphis,[12] but her purpose never wavered. It was all in preparation for her future in Japan.

Others may have forgotten the vow she had made to McCaleb some years earlier, but not Sarah. Once her studies were complete, she sent word: she was ready. And McCaleb expressed his joy in an issue of *Missionary Messenger*, a newsletter he edited from Tokyo with C. G. Vincent: "A young sister, a graduate with a BS degree and now a teacher, writes as follows: 'You remember a few years ago when you were at D[ickson] that a little girl came to you after the last lecture and told you she was going to be a missionary in Japan. I am now twenty-one years old and am making preparations to fulfill this, my greatest desire,'" he reported. "I rejoice to know that our sister has during these years held sacred her vow, and that now, having reached the years of mature womanhood this is still her 'greatest desire.' A nobler resolve could not be made."[13]

CHAPTER THREE

Setting Sail for Far-off Lands

He that goeth forth and weepeth, bearing precious seed,
shall doubtless come again with rejoicing,
bringing his sheaves with him.

PSALM 126:6

The notice was simple enough, published in the August 1915 issue of the *Word and Work* magazine, a journal published by members of Churches of Christ: "Miss Sarah Andrews, of Dickson, Tennessee, who expects to join the workers in Japan next fall. Funds for her passage are asked for, and contributions may be sent to I. B. Bradley, Dickson, Tennessee."[1]

Sarah was now an educated young woman, recognized for "her spirit and her pluck,"[2] and as such, had gathered a small band of support for her impending adventure. I. B. Bradley, who had become the minister of the Walnut Street Church of Christ in 1905,[3] helped Sarah raise $350. McCaleb had asked for contributions on her behalf, as well, calling her "one of the most consecrated women in the Church of Christ."[4] All told, with her own savings included, she had $525, and her father agreed to pay the one-way passage on the boat.[5]

On December 25, 1915, Will Andrews took his twenty-three-year-old daughter to the train depot and watched her board for the far west. Once there, she'd catch the steam liner *Empress of Japan* for the Orient, a journey that wouldn't end until January 16. In a recounting of the trip for the magazine *Missionary Messenger*, she admitted that with the exception of only two days, her sea voyage was "very rough."[6] And yet, there was much for the self-proclaimed "Middle Tennessee girl" to see.

Aboard the train, she found "extremely interesting" scenery between Chicago and Vancouver, British Columbia. "For forty-eight hours after leaving Chicago, we were viewing broad prairies which were quite a novelty," she wrote. "The scenery was greatly changed the last two and half days spent on rail. With a heart filled with reverence and awe, I gazed in wonder at the famous Canadian Rockies, many peaks of which tower thousands of feet in the air."[7]

Sarah spent most of her time in the observation car, where a guide pointed out glaciers, ravines, and more. By this time, Sarah wrote, she had made many acquaintances, including a couple of young ladies who would join her on the *Empress*. "These I found to be very congenial and helpful, one having made the trip to Japan about two years ago."[8]

The train arrived in Vancouver on New Year's Day, where Sarah and the others boarded the ship. The *Empress* was an ocean liner from the Canadian Pacific Line, and it traveled between Vancouver, Hong Kong, and Japan, carrying mail, freight, and passengers at record-breaking speeds. It featured both a steam engine and full masts and rigging, and included luxurious first-class accommodations, but it wasn't quite the same as a trip on one of today's modern cruise lines; up to seven hundred passengers would travel below in steerage.[9]

Sarah was shown her stateroom, only to discover that her roommate was a missionary of eleven years' standing, also bound for Japan. And within a day, they were all "far away on the rolling bosom of the seemingly limitless waters of the mighty Pacific."[10]

But bad storms and a continuous headwind plagued the journey, so much so that the boat would arrive more than twenty-four hours late. Sarah wrote that God was near and dear to her throughout, but others felt the torment.

"On the sea, men who have never made a daily friend of God cry to him in their need," she reported. "As George Herbert said, 'He that will learn to pray let him go to sea.' The 107th Psalm is a marvelous description of a storm at sea. 'They that are at their wits end. Then they cry unto Jehovah.' Yea in dire distress men always cry unto Jehovah for unto whom shall they go for comfort and help save unto Him. We were wonderfully blest!"[11]

McCaleb and others greeted Sarah once she arrived in Yokohama, and she was already acutely aware of just how far she had come. She met many friends on the ship, but none were of a kindred spirit:

> I left home alone so far as human association was concerned, but the promise of the Savior was remembered, "I will never leave thee nor forsake thee." Although I am now far away from loved ones, I am comforted by the words of the poet, "There is a scene where spirits blend/Where friend holds fellowship with friend/Though sunder'd far, by faith we meet/Around the common mercy seat."[12]

Sarah's first years in Japan were spent at the home of McCaleb and his first wife Della, learning the language and customs while teaching English. She admitted more than once that the communication was difficult, and while there she suffered from what she called "nervous trouble" and appendicitis, but that wasn't all; the culture was vastly different from her own Tennessee upbringing. That included the fact that, as she told McCaleb, she had never before experienced so many "curious" smells.[13]

Perphaps suprisingly, however, there were similarities between the cultures. Toyohiko Kagawa, who published a book called *Christ and Japan* in 1934, described his people as pious, loyal, and compassionate, virtues that Sarah could certainly relate to. And yet, he also admitted that they showed a lack of patience and endurance as a whole; that they were averse to criticism of any kind; and that historically, emotions were not to be shown.[14] Kagawa wrote:

> Weeping must be limited to thrice during a lifetime. In their home the children were taught that it was unseemly to laugh in anyone's presence. Especially is laughter rare among our women. Women of the lower classes freely indulge in laughter, but those of the middle classes keep their faces as rigid as the surface of a plaster wall. Even when the occasion calls for laughter, they remain sober as statues. If, peradventure, they yield to the mood and laugh, they hastily cover over their mouths with their hands. They are seemingly concerned lest they mar the harmony of their facial beauty.[15]

> What a pity that the Japanese find laughter so difficult as compared with the ease with which Americans are able to laugh their way through life.[16]

Sarah, by contrast, was described by her family members as being warm, playful, and fun-loving. She had even been awarded medals for dramatic readings as a child.[17] Pictures of her from Japan, solemn-faced and serious, might lead someone to think otherwise. But as she visited relatives back home, they noted that she seemed to have taken on the ways of those she served across the sea.[18]

Apparently, however, her humility and dedication found favor. According to her sister Elizabeth "Bess" Delk, Sarah was able to lead ten people to salvation and baptism during her first year in Japan—and one of those ten would make all the difference in the world.[19] Iki Naemura, whom Sarah would warmly refer to as "Iki-San," would go on to become Sarah's helper, friend, and confidante for the rest of her days.

According to Iki-San's niece, Kuni Nakajima, Iki-San was "so young at heart and cheerful that everybody who came in contact with her loved her very much."[20]

Sarah and Iki-San became like sisters, and in 1919, the pair set out for a new adventure, with Iki-San's mother in tow. They moved to Okitsu, an "untouched" town of less than ten thousand people about one hundred miles southwest of Tokyo.[21]

"We started work by opening a kindergarten, conducting Bible classes in my home, Sunday school for the children, distributing tracts and Bible portions from house to house, calling a native evangelist occasionally for meetings and street preaching, etc.,"[22] Sarah reported to the folks back home. As a woman, Sarah was still somewhat limited in her role, as evidenced by the missionary notes from a December 1916 issue of *Word and Work* magazine. Speaking of the woman who sent money to Sarah and the McCalebs, the article said, "That Texas sister . . . could preach a good missionary sermon if she were a man."[23]

Regardless, the work forged on. Some of the American missionaries—who included the likes of O. D. Bixler, twin brothers Herman and Harry Fox, and E. A. Rhodes—began meeting on Sunday afternoons for services in English, and each saw individual successes. "When the officials asked Sister Andrews to have neither prayer nor Christian songs in her kindergarten, like Daniel of old, she declined to accede," *Word and Work* reported in June 1920. "There were nearly eighty-five applicants, of whom she accepted thirty-two for the first term. 'One of the larger children wept,' Sister Andrews writes, 'when she heard the story of Joseph for the first time. . . . '"[24]

And from another issue, a report from Brother Otoshige Fujimore: "I baptized five at Okitsu; however, it is not my preaching, but their honest work." A series of baptisms had been reported within Sarah's first four months, in fact, including a young girl she was helping through school, a woman of sixty-one, the assistant station master's son, an ex-naval officer, the ex-subchief of a village, a boy of sixteen, and an almost seventy-year-old Presbyterian man. And then there were the eighteen grammar school boys who came to her asking to be taught about Christ, resulting in two evening sessions a week.[25]

Sarah was, according to Bradley, "an untiring, conscientious worker and an efficient missionary."[26] But she was also a woman who needed some rest.

CHAPTER FOUR

To Give and Give Some More

And he said unto me, My grace is sufficient for thee:
for my strength is made perfect in weakness.
Most gladly therefore will I rather glory
in my infirmities, that the power of Christ
may rest upon me.

2 CORINTHIANS 12:9

On December 6, 1920, Sarah Andrews headed home on the ship *Colombia* for a respite, "having accomplished a very fine work in Okitsu."[1] The original plan, as recalled by her sister Bess, was that Sarah would be back in Dickson some five to seven years after her initial journey, and it was almost five years to the day. The time had been busy; in 1920 alone, according to *Word and Work*, the Japanese missionaries had baptized forty-four people,[2]

and those still across the sea could be counted on to continue the work in her absence.

By January of 1922, the same magazine reported that Sarah was eager to return,[3] despite some lingering concern for her health. She had always been slight (some would say frail), but the stresses of her overseas work had already begun to catch up with her. *Word and Work* reported the following spring that Sarah had set sail for Japan, but that her health was "not very good," and therefore, she "should be supplied promptly with the means to provide her a sanitary home. Failure here on our part may shorten her life."[4]

One of the most serious threats was the possibility of tuberculosis, due to industrial expansion and the large number of people living in crowded conditions and working in hot, dusty factories; sick employees were then sent home, spreading the disease even further.[5] An epidemic of influenza in 1918–19 had further weakened immune systems in Japan, causing a sharp rise in deaths from the disease.[6] Since Sarah was set on returning to Japan regardless, she and the other missionaries should at least have an "American-style home" to help protect her, *Word and Work* warned.[7]

The congregants answered the call. In 1924, when Sarah and Iki-San relocated to Shizuoka (an area in the center of Japan with the Pacific Ocean to the south and Mt. Fuji to the northeast), they would find a new definition of "home" in a pre-cut Sears, Roebuck, and Co. house. Sarah's brother, Pete Andrews, had helped in the process. The kit had been ordered, crated, and shipped from the United States. Never mind that the directions arrived in English; the determined missionary took them in hand and translated them to Japanese for her workers—even if there were a few pieces left over when all was said and done.[8]

The house was fairly simple in design, with a few bedrooms, dining room, and kitchen, and by having it as her own, Sarah was decidedly in vogue. Between 1908 and 1940, the mail-order company sold about seventy-five thousand homes, and the 1920s were a peak period. Along with the numbered and stamped lumber, the kits arrived with seven hundred fifty pounds of nails, ten pounds of wood putty, twenty-seven gallons of paint and varnish, four hundred sixty pounds of window weights, and four hundred feet of sash cord.[9]

It was providence that the home didn't arrive a year earlier; on October 1, 1923, an earthquake measuring 8.3 on the Richter scale decimated Tokyo's business and industrial areas, killing almost 100,000 people and displacing many more.[10] Sarah made it through the ordeal unharmed, but McCaleb's house suffered, and another worker's house had burned. Regardless, the missionaries took full advantage of the opportunity: McCaleb, Sarah, and Iki-San distributed clothes and household necessities in addition to Christian tracts.[11]

Though Sarah was considered a "very ambitious missionary,"[12] by mid-1924 *Word and Work* was reporting on several others as well. Some of the couples had gone on to have children, but not Sarah; she remained single. Her sister Bess recalled Sarah had been in love with a young man in faraway Dickson, but after his early death, there was never another man, as far as her family knew.

She did, however, have the support and companionship of other missionaries. In addition to McCaleb (whose wife had returned to the States), there were also Herman and Sarah Fox in Tokyo; E.A. and Bess Rhodes in Ibaraki; Orville and Anna Bixler in Ibaraki; Harry Robert and Pauline Fox in Fukushima; Lillie D. Cypert in Tokyo; Yunosuke Hiratsuka in Tokyo; and Otoshige Fujimore in Shimosa.[13] And back home, congregants received urgent pleas to continue helping them all.

"This is no time to cut down missionary giving," implored one issue of *Word and Work*. "Let us bear in mind it is the privilege and a pleasure to help support the faithful men and women who have gone to the distant fields; that God expects it; that the missionaries will be inconvenienced and the work will suffer if we do not. The cause needs more donors and more donors will come when there is more teaching force. Have you any obligation there? What is it?"[14]

The money came in, but it was irregular at best. For Sarah, there were reports of $50 here, $25 there, and maybe even the occasional $80, all gathered and sent by Bradley. Though the finances were slim, they buoyed Sarah's spirits. "I have never given the last away," she told the folks back home, "that the next ship brought what I needed."[15]

The work in Japan was hard, at best. Though more Americans continued to heed the call and go (and the workers reported converts and baptisms), the ground remained largely fallow. Years later, a newspaper reporter would declare, "It is the opinion of Miss Andrews that it will require decades before great inroads can be made in imperial worship by the Japanese because the teaching of Christianity is a long, difficult struggle."[16] Even so, Sarah wrote friends, "This is work in hard places, but God's grace is ever sufficient. There is an eternal purpose in this service that gives inward courage and joy even when outward results appear discouraging and sometime grievous."[17]

The challenge was in the fact that the Japanese were already a spiritual people—they just didn't see the need to subscribe to a particular religion. In *Christ and Japan*, Toyohiko Kagawa wrote:

> Had Christianity recognized the points of merit in Japanese Buddhism and not taken such a firm and uncompromising attitude, the latter faith would have reciprocated by treating Christianity as a revelation of one of the gods of the pantheistic pantheon and Christ as one of the gods of mercy. In a Buddhist temple in the city of Kobe, the figure of Christ is actually

worshipped under the title of Christ the God of Mercy. There are also instances where Buddhist temples celebrate Christ's birthday, calling the occasion Buddhist Christmas.[18]

The Christian idea of the narrow gate and the admonition of Jesus as the only way to the Father, then, flew in the face of traditional Japanese tolerance. "In Japan, both Shinto and Buddhist believers frequent Christian churches and attend weddings and funerals held under Christian auspices," Kagawa wrote in 1934. "Thus, when Christians refuse to reciprocate by attending Shinto and Buddhist functions of this character, it creates a most unfortunate impression."[19]

Discouragement constantly knocked at the door. And that wasn't all. Sarah, once again, found herself challenged by her health.

CHAPTER FIVE

No Short Trip

Therefore take no thought, saying, What shall
we eat? or, What shall we drink? or, Wherewithal
shall we be clothed? (For after all these things
do the Gentiles seek:) for your heavenly Father
knoweth that ye have need of all these things.
But seek ye first the kingdom of God, and his
righteousness; and all these things
shall be added unto you.

MATTHEW 6:31–33

By mid–1925, the word being circulated was that Sarah Andrews was seriously sick and might have to return from the field. "I may have to go [home] and will if it seems best later on," Sarah wrote, "though as far as my wishes are concerned I would love to go to heaven from Japan."[1]

But a year later, Sarah was still soldiering on. She did give up her class work for the summer, though, allowing her to do some writing and studying. "Guess I was more tired than I realized," she wrote home, "for since I have freedom from class responsibility my appetite is better and I may be gaining weight. The Lord is good to me."[2]

Apparently, so was Iki-San; "She had a sick spell recently and I felt my right hand was gone."[3]

Within a few months, however, the pair had decided to return home. Hettie Lee Ewing, another American missionary, would fill in while they were gone.[4] Fortunately, missionary Harry Robert Fox and his family would come to stay in Sarah's house, as it would be no short trip.

Iki-San would later recall that she and Sarah spent time in both Nashville and Dickson as well as two and a half years in Los Angeles. While there, they helped a Japanese church and learned skills that could be useful back in Japan, like dressmaking, cooking, and the like.[5] It wasn't until September 1930 that Sarah and Iki-San were on the way back to Japan, and they were well received indeed.

"We have so many callers together with the regular work, I find it hard to settle myself to writing," Sarah reported in early 1931. "I think I'll have to take two or three days off every three or four months and go off to some quiet place and write, write, write. I'm glad indeed that the Japanese feel free to call—wouldn't have it otherwise."[6]

Sarah and Iki-San were back in Shizuoka then, and the work had continued to expand. With the support of the people back home, they would go on to build several churches in the area, "not unmindful, however, that the devil is ever busy and may at any time stir up strife, if we are not diligent in prayer."[7] Brothers in the faith would visit and preach, helping share the burden. But there was another challenge that plagued them all: a lack of funds.

In March 1933, the U.S. banking crisis (set off by the stock market crash of 1929) had come to a head, and the ripples crossed the ocean.[8] For Sarah and her contemporaries, the crisis meant that funds given for the work were deposited into a Dickson bank that had closed. I. B. Bradley, still handling donations for her, had done his best to cover the contributions, but told her that he wasn't sure when he would have anything to send again. There was still no regular church support.[9]

"Of course, this loss is a blow to the work and our plans," Sarah wrote, "but we are trying to make the best of the situation and trusting in God's promises. For the sake of the donors I regret very much that your offerings were lost, but I believe you understand the situation and will not be discouraged."[10]

Sarah herself was still fighting discouragement in regard to her health. The same letter expressed her joy at the addition of capable workers in her ministry, saying she was "thankful indeed, for I fear I am not physically able to continue at the present rate."[11] There was just so much to do. Ewing, reporting from the Miyamoto-Cho area of Tokyo, sent word of numerous baptisms and a Sunday school that numbered more than one hundred each Sunday, plus a church membership of sixteen. "Considering there was no Christian teaching in this section of the city until we began here a little more than one year ago, we feel that the Lord has surely blessed our efforts," she wrote.[12] There were also reports of house-to-house work, confessions, and inquiries in other Japanese areas. The same year, efforts began in Shimizu, a large port town that was part of the Shizuoka Prefecture. At the time, it had a population of seventy-five thousand, and within a few years, a chapel would be built to further solidify the Christian endeavors.[13]

Just as Sarah celebrated the expansion, however, she also dealt with tremendous loss. Her dear father, William Thomas Andrews, died on September 23, 1934, at the age of seventy-four. He was more than simply a man who saw his daughter off at the train station all those years ago; according to information his family presented for his obituary, he was also one who "displayed an independence of thought and courage to follow the dictates of his convictions. [This] was characteristic of his forebearers, who were among the early settlers of the Jamestown Colony of Virginia, [who] left their home in London, England, seeking religious freedom in the New World. . . . The beautiful simplicity which marked his life prevailed unto the end."[14]

The apple apparently didn't fall too far from the tree.

Of course, Sarah was far from alone in her challenges; the other missionaries had struggles, too. A single article in *Word and Work* told of the loss of Sarah's father, as well as spinal trouble, sciatica, poisoning, malaria, regional indifference, a tonsil operation, flu approaching pneumonia, eye trouble, fourteen days of fever, and more among the saints overseas.[15]

"Yet with all the foregoing ills there is not a single missionary who is willing to abandon his field and work," wrote the article's author, Don Carlos Janes. His words turned out to be vain hope. Within six months, there was word that Harry Fox had suffered for years with a malady incurable in Japan and was advised to return home. And as for Sarah? She was in need of an operation.[16] A student of David Lipscomb College in Nashville, Tokuo Mazawa, prepared to travel to Japan in her stead and keep the work going. By then, Sarah's churches included nearly four hundred in Sunday schools, and three of the churches had their own buildings. "Sister Andrews has labored long and faithfully, handicapped with a frail body; but she has accomplished more than any other missionary the church has on the foreign field," Brother R. S. King, a Church of Christ preacher, wrote to *Word and Work* magazine. "Truly she is one of God's great women."[17]

CHAPTER SIX

Ashes of the Dead

Thou shalt have no other gods before me.
Thou shalt not make unto thee any graven image,
or any likeness of any thing that is in heaven above,
or that is in the earth beneath, or that is
in the water under the earth:
Thou shalt not bow down thyself to them,
nor serve them: for I the LORD thy God
am a jealous God, visiting the iniquity
of the fathers upon the children unto the third
and fourth generation of them that hate me;
And shewing mercy unto thousands of them
that love me, and keep my commandments.

EXODUS 20:3–6

*W*hile Sarah underwent medical treatment in the States—family members recall that they included a stint at the Mayo Clinic—Japan was going through challenges of its own. By the time Sarah returned in 1939, the country was nothing like she had left it. In her absence, the nation had become part of the burgeoning drift toward the Second World War. She wasn't quite herself, either; family members protested her trip, fearing that between her health and the war, she'd never make it back to the States alive. She wrote:

> The pall of war hung over the land, with its black-outs, strict police force, scarcity of commodities, soldiers everywhere, the odor of ammunition factories filling the air. Occasional long lines of soldiers could be seen, each bearing a tiny, white box containing the remains of dead comrades being taken for enshrinement to a national shrine where the spirits of those who fall for their country are believed to repose. These boxes did not always contain the ashes of the dead, but more frequently only some personal effect or perhaps a lock of hair which had been left by its owner to be thus enshrined in the event of the inevitable. And not least noticeable were the weird and loud chantings before the god shelf day and night for the safety of the member of the family at the battle front. Indeed, evidences of the burden and sorrows of the war were everywhere depressing.[1]

The situation was made even worse by a destructive fire that wiped out large portions of Shizuoka in 1940; Sarah and the others escaped harm, but the church work multiplied while they cared for refugees.[2]

There was something else weighing heavy on Sarah's mind: talk had begun of the "Kyodan," which was to be a united Church of Christ in Japan, and it didn't sit well with her at all. She later recalled:

The religious law which was being framed by the government and the vacillating condition of the Churches of Christ under pressure of state were of paramount concern to me. I began immediately to make a study of the law and to correct erroneous trends in the churches by taking up a study of the New Testament church with some of the members in my home.

[The Japanese government was] undertaking to unite all phases of national enterprises in an endeavor to tighten its hold on everything in the islands. Consequently the Department of Education, having the supervision of religious matters, undertook to unify religion under three heads—namely, Shinto, Buddhist, and Christian—eliminating all division and sects in each. As regards the Christian religion, this law not only combined church and state, but set up a superorganization to which all groups of the Christian faith were requested to adhere.[3]

Missionaries were given no say in the matter, Sarah reported, and told only that the new Christian arm of the effort would be called "The Japanese Christian Church." Sarah wrote:

The Churches of Christ were faced with a grave situation. I endeavored to impress upon the members that if the churches entered such a federation, they ceased thereupon to be Churches of Christ. I encouraged them to stand for the New Testament order and trust God for the consequences, even if they were ordered to disband and must worship God in secret as in days of old Rome. The three churches where I labored were determined to do that very thing, when suddenly one of the leaders became a veritable turncoat and began making a strong and arduous attempt with clandestine tactics to take these churches into this national union. My heart was burdened, and prayers and tears went up to God for Zion's cause.[4]

Sarah, it turns out, wasn't the only one contemplating a potential loss of denominational legacy, or worse. The government's philosophy required the people to worship the emperor as a living god, and a Religious Bodies Law passed in 1939 allowed the government to censor religious organizations.

According to a report on Baptist history and heritage, the law also allowed the government to interfere in the business affairs of religious organizations, including ordering most religious groups "to submit detailed reports of almost every business matter, such as erecting new buildings and appointing new leadership. All these attempts were aimed at crushing a sense of religious liberty and shattering every form of antinationalistic sentiment among the people, especially churches of various Christian denominations."[5]

Today, it might be difficult to understand why any religious organization might go along with such tactics, but many did; it was part of cooperating with the state as "good Japanese citizens," and believing—incorrectly—that going along with the rules might keep them from further trouble.[6] According to the same report, some 218,370 members from a variety of denominational churches united to form the Kyodan in 1941—even though "no sufficient preparation or theological consensus concerning church order and a confession of faith existed" during the formation. "Therefore, getting harmony among participating denominations was difficult from the beginning." It wasn't just the Church of Christ—or Sarah—raising a fuss; other denominations, such as the Evangelical Lutheran Church and the Presbyterian-related Japanese Christian Church, weren't happy, either.[7]

As time went on, even those who joined the federation discovered that it wouldn't mean smooth sailing. Persecution grew. Some missionaries were interrogated as suspected spies; others who were outspoken enough were imprisoned and tortured for disrespecting the emperor and demonstrating anti-nationalism.[8]

Not surprisingly, missionaries began to return home. A *Time* magazine article from December 1941 reported that there were only ninety Protestant missionaries in Japan at that time, compared to six hundred forty the year prior.[9]

Even among Sarah's associates, many had packed up for the States. By 1942, according to *Word and Work*, McCaleb was in California; Herman Fox was in Kentucky, and the Rhodes family was working with a church in Long Beach, California.[10]

But Sarah, along with fellow missionary Lillie Cypert, would remain.

"The international situation was becoming more tense," Sarah would later recall when American nationals were advised to evacuate. "But I was not afraid; besides, the cause was at stake, so I had no thought of leaving."[11]

Sarah would be tested further on December 7, 1941, when the Japanese executed a surprise attack on the Americans at Pearl Harbor. Believing that the U.S. battleship force could be a threat to the expansion of the empire, the Japanese waged an incredible assault. Coming in two waves, Japanese forces killed or wounded 3,581 American military; killed or injured 103 civilians; sank five battleships and damaged three more; sank three cruisers and three destroyers; and destroyed 188 planes and damaged 155 more.[12]

Sarah, suddenly finding herself in a different level of enemy territory, received the news early in the morning the day after the attack. "A neighbor came telling me that war had been declared between our countries," she wrote.[13]

And just two days later, she was summoned by the police.

CHAPTER SEVEN

A Foretaste of Heaven

Fear thou not; for I am with thee: be not dismayed;
for I am thy God: I will strengthen thee;
yea, I will help thee; yea, I will uphold thee
with the right hand of my righteousness.

ISAIAH 41:10

*T*he days that followed would be darker than Sarah, or anyone back home, could have imagined. When the police arrived at her door, they didn't come to simply ask questions; they came to give orders. She was told to discontinue all teaching and "warned regarding other movements," she later wrote.[1]

Sarah deeply regretted the loss of her Bible study class, but made the most of it all the same:

There was a service I could render even in internment. It was in his loneliness and exile John had the glorious visions of his Redeemer, and it was in prison that Paul wrote many of the New Testament letters. In this period of forced seclusion, I saw an opportunity for preparing these Bible-study topics to be printed in pamphlet form for the Japanese. This I determined to do if indeed my books were not confiscated.[2]

Sarah was ordered to submit a list of everything she owned to the Finance Department, "even to the number of pocket handkerchiefs." She wrote:

One of the police asked why I had more than one copy of the Bible. The police did not take my Bible, but he did take the manuscripts of "Notes on Galatians and Ephesians," which I had ready for translation and printing. I had devoted much time to this work, and was sorry indeed to lose it, because the Japanese need Bible-study helps. Happily, I finished "Bible-Study Topics" before being sent to concentration camp in September 1942, and left them with a Japanese Christian for translation.[3]

And yes, Sarah did say concentration camp. Apparently, the simple monitoring of her activities hadn't been enough. That fall, she and three Catholic women from Shizuoka were sent to a camp in Yokohama. They boarded a train for a one-hundred-mile trip, guarded by four police—one for each of the prisoners.[4]

The Japanese treatment of Sarah, it should be noted, was not that different from the way Japanese immigrants were handled in the United States. Just two months after the raid on Pearl Harbor, President Franklin D. Roosevelt issued Executive Order 9066, which gave the American military the right to exclude any person from any designated area. The country wanted the Japanese off the west coast, and it began with a "voluntary evacuation." Before long, however, that evacuation was no longer a mere suggestion; anyone of Japanese descent—whether an American citizen or not—was shipped off to a temporary assembly center and then a relocation area further inland. They were allowed to bring only what they could carry, and many established businessmen and farmers who had long lived in the U.S. lost their properties. There were ten such relocation areas in various states, and each held between 8,000 and 16,000 detainees; all in all, more than 100,000 Japanese—including women and children—were held, even though some 70,000 of them were U.S. citizens.[5]

Public opinion of the Japanese, with the help of pro-war propaganda, reached new lows. The folks back home wouldn't just fear for Sarah's safety—they would also wonder if she was indeed still alive. Much like her imprisoned counterparts back in the States, Sarah had limited ability to communicate with family and friends. And this would last for years.

Bettie Lundy, Sarah's niece, remembers her father's stories about those dark days, the challenge not to imagine the worst. The reality, however, was that things really were that bad. Sarah wasn't dead, but she was certainly suffering.

They had been aware of her health challenges, the illnesses and weakness that had left her hospitalized and working from her bed, giving directions to her helpers.[6] They had seen her return to the States even more frail than when she had left, and heard the advice of the doctors advising her to stay in America and take up a more simple life. But they also knew she was a woman of conviction, one whose determination would override the frustrations of an almost fifty-year-old body that didn't work like she wanted it to.

But there, in the Yokohama concentration camp, her frailty once again reared its ugly head; it was a mere two weeks before her health was so bad that she was ordered back home under house arrest.

"My sudden return from camp was a sore disappointment to those who were striving to enter the federation and to those who were eager for my property," she later wrote. "It would have been easy to take over this enemy national's property if only the enemy national were not occupying her home."[7]

Sarah firmly believed that she was being tortured based on her stance against joining the united church. For her to do so would have meant denying her heritage and upbringing, going all the way back to the days when her beloved parents helped start the little Walnut Street Church of Christ. She stood firm, even amid the persecution.

And yes, the persecution came. She had been ordered to solitary confinement at her home, watched by guards, and they did whatever they could do—including various "schemes, plottings and trickery" to get her back out so all of her property would be lost.[8]

She wrote:

> The police and guards at the gate joined in trying to make a riddance of me. Those interested first undertook to prove that I was not sick and should be returned to [the] concentration camp. When this failed, the next attempt was to send me to a sanitarium. Then, on account of the bombings, they appealed to the government to evacuate me to the mountains. The next attempt to get me out was to accuse me of committing an offense against the government and to send me to prison. Lastly, they pronounced me insane and arrangements got underway to send me to an asylum in Manchuria. This is funny now, but believe me, it was gruesome then.[9]

It would be decades before the organizers of the Kyodan would recognize—and ask forgiveness for—the "mistakes" made during World War II. In 1967, Masahisa Suzuki, moderator of the Nihon Kirisuto Kyodan (a large Protestant body in Japan), wrote:

Indeed, even as our country committed sin, so we too, as a church, fell into the same sin. We neglected to perform our mission as a "watchman." Now, with deep pain in our hearts, we confess our sin and ask the Lord for forgiveness. We also seek the forgiveness of the peoples of all nations, particularly in Asia, and of the church therein and of our brothers and sisters in Christ throughout the world; as well as the forgiveness of the people in our own country.[10]

Sarah, however, didn't need the confession at that moment. What she needed the most was the continued hand of provision and sustenance from the Lord her God—and the faithful servant received it.

Sarah recalled:

I was forced to live alone during the last two years of the war, and food was very scarce. My garden space was confiscated, so that I could not grow vegetables. The loneliness, the starvation, the pressure, the tormentings could not have been endured but for the consciousness of God's presence and power. Indeed, to be left alone without God would be too awful for words, but to be left alone with God is a foretaste of heaven. I knew that God is faithful, who will not suffer us to be tried above that we are able to bear. I trusted in the exceeding greatness of his power toward us who believe, and in the promise: "The eyes of the Lord run to and fro throughout the whole earth to show himself strong in the behalf of those whose hearts are perfect toward him."[11]

Rather than turning her against God, wondering why she had to endure such hardships, Sarah said she learned to love Jesus more for his sufferings.

"Paul said: 'Therefore I take pleasure in being without strength, in insults, in being pinched, in being chased about, in being cooped up in a corner for Christ's sake,'" she wrote. She knew that it was more about the war and the federation than it was about her personally, so weak legs and all, she continued to stand.[12]

CHAPTER EIGHT

The Great Commission
Reaches Japan

Go ye therefore, and teach all nations,
baptizing them in the name of the Father,
and of the Son, and of the Holy Ghost:
Teaching them to observe all things whatsoever I
have commanded you: and, lo, I am with you always,
even unto the end of the world. Amen.

MATTHEW 28:19–20

*T*hough Protestant churches (the Church of Christ among them) would claim missions work in Japan began in the 1800s, the country's history with Christianity went back centuries earlier. Some believe that Nestorian missionaries—who taught that Jesus had two persons, one human and one divine[1]—arrived from other Asian countries as far back as 199 AD, planting Japan's first churches over the next two hundred years.[2]

It is generally more accepted, however, that a Jesuit priest named Francis Xavier introduced Christian concepts to Japan in 1549. Overseas Missionary Fellowship (OMF), formerly known as the China Inland Mission and founded in 1865, reports that Xavier's "stamina, zeal, and willingness to suffer resulted in thousands of conversions in just two short years."[3] Xavier is considered a saint by the Catholic Church, not to mention the greatest missionary since the time of the apostles.[4]

But challenges followed Xavier's debut. In coming years, in order to make inroads with the Japanese, the growing church began incorporating Shinto and Buddhist practices in worship, as well as:

> . . . using feudal lords to coerce their subjects to convert. The shoguns were also eventually persuaded that Christianity was an attempt to soften them up for European conquest. Added to that, quarrels among rival missionary groups aggravated the situations and as a result, as many as 280,000 Japanese Christians were persecuted and thousands were martyred.[5]

Not surprisingly, Japan banned Christianity in 1626 and the government did everything possible to root out any remaining believers and force them to denounce their faith. A newsletter from the International Affairs section of Nagasaki's City Hall would later tell stories of oppression in that time period, such as the system of the five-household neighborhood unit. According to the article:

> This system required five people to watch each other and all residents to have collective responsibility for any occurrences in their neighborhoods. The other policy was a system of the "temple

guarantee," which required all families to be parishioners of a Buddhist temple, and show proof of their membership. They were also required to have the priest of their family temple chant at burial services and to inscribe posthumous Buddhist names on their tombstones.[6]

And that's not all. There was also the renowned practice of *fumie*, which meant "trampling on the picture." Suspected Christians were forced to trample on images of the Virgin Mary—sacred to those Catholic converts—to prove they were not of the faith. Those that were exposed were forced to convert to Buddhism, and if they wouldn't, were eventually put to death. Some Christians sought refuge in the woods, but government officials set fire to the woods in order to flush them out.[7]

Christianity, then, remained an underground effort for the next two hundred thirty years. But in the mid-1800s, thanks to the Kanagawa Treaty, a shift occurred. Japan ended its two-century-old isolationist foreign policy known as *Sakoku*, through which the entrance or exit of the country was punishable by death. The treaty, signed on March 31, 1854, opened the country's ports—and brave missionaries were headed to the newly accessible country within a handful of years.

McCaleb and his Church of Christ group arrived in 1892, and like previous missionaries from other denominations, believed that offering education was the way into the Japanese people's souls. And it was in that year, across the ocean, that future missionary and teacher Sarah Andrews was born.

As the days of Sarah's house arrest persisted, the reality continued: she was a bona fide enemy of the state, and since the war was going against the Japanese, the people were desperate. She later wrote:

Some friends surmised that I was fed by the Japanese government or through Red Cross channels. Others thought that my needs were taken care of from Brother McCaleb's funds in Japan. Still others thought I had died. None of these surmises are correct.[8]

The reality was that American assets in Japan had been frozen since 1941, in addition to the suspension of the postal service. After Sarah used all of the funds she had available, she was forced to sell her furniture piece by piece to buy food. She recalled:

All enemy property was held by the Finance Department as confiscable; hence, to obtain permission to use any of it required excessive official routine or red tapery. I was required to get permission to sell each piece of furniture, then permission again to use the money. Although the amount I was permitted each month was only a pittance, it was sufficient to pay for my rations, because food and all commodities were scarce. The food situation over there became more and more critical as the war progressed.[9]

Even before she was put under house arrest, then, Sarah had endured lean, lean years.

"I had never experienced hunger until I was caught in throes of war and famine as an enemy national during this war," she wrote. Her weight dropped to a frightfully low seventy-five pounds, and her body swelled from the malnutrition:

In desperation I boiled leaves from the trees for food, boiled and used water from cornstalks for sugar, used sea water for salt, and after months of meatless days I relished grasshoppers for meat, wishing I could have the same dish often. The question comes from many friends: "Why did you stay?" The all-important and satisfying answer to me is that the hand of the Lord was in it all. I learned that once a Christian sees by the eye of faith a controlling purpose, death loses its fears. If I had not been in Japan, it is evident that the three churches in my section of the country, together with the property, would have been lost to the national federation of churches. Therefore, I rejoice to have stayed and suffered for the cause of truth.[10]

CHAPTER NINE

Dark Days and Long Nights

*J*n 1942, the Japanese Empire was at its peak, following a series of successful invasions. But the United States and its allies had already sided with Japan's enemies instead; after the attack on Pearl Harbor, the official word from America was "war."

Sarah, however, would go through her period of house arrest with no full knowledge of the destruction taking place. She would not hear full details of the victories, the defeats, and the atrocities that surrounded her. All she knew was that, as the years went on, the sounds of B-29s overhead increased. And as Japan began losing ground, the people became more and more anxious.

"All the cities and larger towns were being destroyed," she later wrote. "From my home on the outskirts of the city I saw the raid on a neighboring town and two raids on the outskirts of the city where I lived."[1]

Even so, Sarah kept to her work as much as she could. She recalled the writings she had handed off to the Japanese sister for translation at the time she went to the concentration camp.

"When the bombings became intense, [the writings] were placed in a basket of clothing and evacuated to a large warehouse up north," Sarah wrote. She later discovered that the basket had been destroyed during the war, and she deeply regretted the loss.[2]

Sarah realized the great need for literature in Japan and was determined to try again. During her time of confinement, she was "emboldened to attempt to compile a history of the church," although she was fully conscious of her limitations in doing so. "I got this history about half finished when the strain and stress and starvation made it impossible for me to complete it," she remembered.[3] And no doubt, the soldiers that kept her under constant surveillance didn't help.

Family members would later recall stories about the way the soldiers would torment Sarah by banging on her walls day and night. The noises were aggravating, and likely kept her up for hours on end until she became accustomed to the sounds. But all the same, they may have helped prepare her for one of the most significant nights of her life.

It was June 1945, just months after American forces had invaded Iwo Jima and then Okinawa. The United States had

Above: An Andrews family portrait when Sarah had just entered her teens, taken at their home. Standing from left to right: Sarah; Myrtle; Rob; Pete (B. B.); her father, William Thomas; and her mother, Ada (Adele) S. Andrews. The three children in the front are Kate, Douglas, and Bess. The photo was made not long before the house burned to the ground around 1905.

Right: Sarah just before she left Dickson, Tennessee, for Japan on Christmas Day in 1915. She arrived in Japan in January 1916 at the age of twenty-three to fulfill the vow she had made as a young girl.

Right: I. B. Bradley, Sarah's treasurer. Bradley, who had become the minister of the Walnut Street Church of Christ in 1905, helped Sarah raise $350 for her first mission trip and served as her treasurer throughout most of her journeys. *Below:* Walnut Street Church of Christ, Dickson, Tennessee. This building was erected in 1911. The church was started by Sarah's parents and others in 1890 in space above the Dickson Bank and Trust Company.

J. M. McCaleb's home in Japan where missionaries lived while learning the Japanese language and customs. Sarah's first years in Japan were spent at the home of McCaleb and his first wife, Della. This photo was found in a scrapbook kept by McCaleb to record his mission work. Written on the back is "Live with the boys. My room is up 3rd story."

Right: *An early portrait of Sarah and Iki Naemura. Sarah led ten people to salvation and baptism during her first year in Japan. One of those ten, "Iki-San," would go on to become Sarah's helper for the rest of her days.*

Below: *The SS* Colombia. *On December 6, 1920, Sarah headed to the United States on the* Colombia *after working in Okitsu, almost five years to the day that she had left Dickson. The* Colombia *is a sister ship to the SS* Flying Scud, *the freighter that Sarah sailed on from California to Yokohama in May 1949.*

*Sarah and Iki-San. This portrait was made in
Shizuoka after they returned from the United States.*

Right: Sarah and Iki-San from the 1920s. Sarah is dressed in a kimono. The woman on the right is unidenitfied.
Below: Sarah's home in Shizuoka, a pre-cut Sears, Roebuck, and Co. house.

Formal portrait of Sarah in a kimono and sash in Kubota, Japan.

THE SHIZUOKA PREFECTURAL GOVERNMENT

RECOMMENDATION

May 1, 1946

Miss Sera Andrews was born in Dickson City, Tennessee State, U.S.A., She has been a devout christian ever since her childhood. She came over to Japan in January 1916, bent on preaching the Gospel to the Japanese. She had lived in Tokyo for 3years studying Japanese language and manners.

It was in 1919 when she came to Okitsu-machi, where she starred her career devoted to socil work. She opened a public nursery house in Okitsu and held women's societies in Okitsu and its neighbluring villages in order to enlighten Japanese females there, as will as to preach the Gospel to them. In 1939 and 1921, she built at her own expense churches in Okitsu and Shizuoka city.

Indeed, throughout the 30 years that she has been here, her career has been wholly devoted to social work, such as the preaching of the Gospel, managing of Kindergärten, and relief of the sick and the helpless.

She has often suffered insufficient funds for her work and went home to America three times to raise the necessary funds, while she herself has been living in contented poverty, which fact is making a deep impression upon people about her.

Now she has in contemplation another great work with a view to an aid to rebuiding Japan _____ establishment of sanatoriums for the weak.

She is so eager to see her new plan realized that she is again intending to go back to her home America, in order to have the necessary fund ready by appealing for contribution there.

Otherwise, she has sold some estate and buildings of her own, for and to the Seiryo Girls' School that was destroyed by late bombardment. The amount of the reanfer price has been deposited in the bank with whom she has an account The money also goes toward the funds. All tells her ardent religions sentiment.

We enthusiastically hope that this ardent wish of her is fulfiled soon for the good of Japan.

In these views, we beg to herby recommend that you would please favour her with reliesing the amount of cash money required by her from her account freezed.

K. Morita

K. MORITA

Director of Welfare Department,

Shizuoka Prefectural Government.

Official recommendation of the Shizuoka Prefectural Government. Sarah discovered that because so many believed her dead, there had been almost a total discontinuance of funds for her since 1943, and her accounts had been frozen. In May 1946, the director of the Welfare Department of the Shizuoka Prefectural Government made this recommendation for the release of any of her money.

Front view of Okitsu Church of Christ in Shizuoka.

A Christian wedding. Sarah held study groups and even weddings inside her home in Shizuoka.

Church of Christ building in Numazu. Sarah moved from Shizuoka to Numazu in June 1954.

Sarah in 1954, showing her true spirit with a casual pose and warm smile in Japan.

A family portrait during Sarah's later visits to the United States. Back row from left to right: Mark, Nell, Bess, Kate, and Douglas. Front row from left to right: Rob, Pete (B. B.), Myrtle, and Sarah.

Sarah in the 1960s. Made not long before her death in 1961, this photo reveals how years of malnutrition and stress affected not only her weight, but also her teeth, hair, and eyes.

The sixth memorial meeting for Sarah Andrews on October 10, 1967. This picture was taken in front of her memorial and passed down from Iki-San.

Sarah's memorial, dedicated in 1981, twenty years after her death. One hundred Japanese attended the memorial service marking the anniversary.

An epitaph of Sarah Andrews.

Right: Sarah's coworker, Iki-San, in
her later years.
Below: On the left, Koichiro "Tom"
Tamura, senior vice president and
general manager of Sumitomo
Corporation of Japan in Dickson,
visiting the Sarah Andrews gravesite
in Japan.

already celebrated Victory in Europe Day, but Japan had declared it would fight to the end rather than surrender.

The bombing raids had started, and on the night of June 19, the city in their sights was Shizuoka (where Sarah was living in her little Sears, Roebuck, and Co. house). She was, by all accounts, the last of her missionary contemporaries to remain; even Lillie Cypert, who had interned for a year in Tokyo, had returned home.[4]

That night, 123 B-29s bombed the city, and it was an attack filled with death. Aside from the bombs themselves—which took the lives of 2,000 residents and decimated Shizuoka—two of the planes collided, killing 23 of the American crew members.[5]

But just like when Jesus slept through the storm aboard a small fishing boat, Sarah slumbered through the assault.

"I slept peacefully through it all, although bombs were dropped and houses burned within sixty feet of my home," she recalled. "It was no doubt a blessing that I slept, because had I waked and attempted to flee, I probably would have been mobbed, for the feeling was high at that crisis."[6]

Her own feelings were high, too, including frustration at the senseless deaths:

> Many civilians were killed and many more were wounded in the city that night, and needlessly so, for the American army, as was the case before raids on every city, sent planes in advance and dropped circulars warning the people to evacuate. But these warnings were not permitted to get into the hands of the populace.[7]

Sarah, however, wouldn't have time to dwell on the matter. The morning after the bombings, the Japanese were at her door. Her

home was one of few left standing, after all, and she was ordered
to help care for the wounded. She later wrote:

> Seventeen casualties were brought into my house. The chapel
> [which had been built on the front part of her lot] was used a
> clinic. I did my best, but the food supply was so scarce and I was
> so weak that after a fortnight, I broke down and the city moved
> these patients out. My body was swelling, which is one sign of
> starvation, and I was so weak I could not stay up.[8]

New challenges appeared even after the casualties left; Sarah's
house was infested with fleas in a way she'd never before experienced. Enduring her own private hell, she still knew nothing of
what was going on outside her doors—including the dropping of
the atomic bombs on Hiroshima and Nagasaki, with death counts
estimated at more than two hundred thousand.

Sarah later recalled learning of the end of the war:

> But about the middle of August, I noticed that B-29s were not
> coming over. A little later, the woman who delivered my little
> allotment of food told me that the war had ended, that their
> emperor in sympathy for his people had graciously delivered
> them. It was reported that as soon as the emperor finished his
> broadcast at the cessation of arms, the people, being so war-torn
> and weary, relaxed and lay down wherever they were, whether
> on the street or elsewhere, and went to sleep.[9]

By the end of September—after a series of continued surren-
ders by Japanese forces in other parts of the world—things had
changed dramatically. Sarah later wrote in the *Gospel Advocate* of
the end of the war:

The police had come telling me that overtures for peace had been made, my tormenters had fled, foxholes everywhere were being filled, a very fine Japanese lady and her daughter (refugees from Tokyo's destruction) had come to occupy the home with me, food was delivered to me by the Japanese government, Christian Japanese called to see me freely, church services were resumed, and I began to realize that the dark curtain of war had lifted and liberation had come.[10]

As Sarah's strength returned, she even began venturing from the house. But what she saw defied description: only "a fringe of the city," she wrote, was left. And the chapel that had been built in Shimizu had been destroyed.[11]

CHAPTER TEN

The Dawn of a New Day

I will lift up mine eyes unto the hills, from whence
cometh my help. My help cometh from the Lord,
which made heaven and earth. He will not suffer
thy foot to be moved: he that keepeth thee will not slumber.
Behold, he that keepeth Israel shall neither
slumber nor sleep. The Lord is thy keeper: the Lord is thy shade
upon thy right hand. The sun shall not smite thee by day,
nor the moon by night. The Lord shall preserve thee
from all evil: he shall preserve thy soul. The Lord shall preserve
thy going out and thy coming in from this time forth,
and even for evermore.

PSALM 121:1–8

*B*ack home, endless days and months passed with no word from
Sarah. Some felt certain that she would have succumbed to
her illnesses, to the climate, to the stress, or to the simple day-to-day
business of war. But others—especially those in her closest family—
held out hope for Sarah's safe return.

But they didn't just pray. They did whatever they could to locate
her, sending letters that never arrived and checking on every possible
lead. Sarah's sister Myrtle Thompson was living in Tyler, Texas, at the
time and her husband, T. B., was preaching at a church nearby. There
was an army base close enough that soldiers would attend services on
Sundays, and the Thompsons would welcome them home for Sunday
dinner. Myrtle, however, wouldn't just serve up a meal; she'd share
her pride and concern for her sister. Every time a soldier left her
home, he would do so with a card that included Sarah's name and
address and a plea to look for her should he ever get to Japan.[1]

One Sunday, a woman at church shared that her husband, then
in the Pacific, was being sent to Japan with the occupation forces.
Myrtle didn't skip a beat. She received the address for the woman's
husband, William Billingsley, and wrote him with an urgent appeal
to find Sarah. And that he did; her home was located between two
zones of American occupation.

According to newspaper reports, Billingsley, a fellow member
of his company, and a couple of Japanese men headed for Sarah's
home, skirting the military police along the way. They found her
at a church about ten miles from the house. They were the first
American soldiers she had seen, even though U.S. forces had been
stationed not that far away.[2]

The men left her all the rations they had and promised to return
with more. But once the men returned to camp and word spread,
"more" turned into a full Jeep's worth of food and supplies.

"You can imagine my surprise and joy," Sarah wrote Myrtle on October 29, 1945, the day after the soldiers arrived. "I was so happy I felt almost as if I was having a real visit with the homefolks."[3]

The soldiers gave her the latest news from home, and helped her share her own adventures with them, too. During the war, Sarah later recalled, she had received only three, twenty-five-word letters from her mother through Red Cross channels; the limited word count was set for correspondence of those who were interned, and even those precious few phrases would be censored before being sent on.

"It was so kind of these gentlemen to make the long, hard trip over the mountain in their truck-like car to find me," she continued in the letter to her sister. "Of course, the homefolks will appreciate it as well as I. I read and re-read your letters and really digested them after the friends had gone."[4]

Sarah admitted surprise that none of her letters had reached the home front, since she wrote more twenty-five-word pieces in the previous year than at any other time during the war. To her sister, Sarah wrote:

> One such letter every two months was permitted, and I sent several, but I suppose conditions were such that it was impossible to get them through either by boat or plane. You say I have not been heard from since May 1944 and you have tried every way to get in touch with me. That's just like you to make the utmost effort in behalf of "my folks." Ha![5]

Sarah was obviously giddy at the newly opened lines of communication. At the same time, she was well aware of the stress that her absence had likely caused the ones she loved. "I am so sorry to have been the cause of making you all so anxious, especially to have had Mother worry," she wrote. "But I remember her great faith and that gave her abiding comfort."[6]

Sarah also reported that her health was better than it had been since earlier in the year, and that she was making plans to come home as soon as the government and her doctor deemed it acceptable.

But then, even after all she had been through, she shared further surprising news: she wouldn't be coming home to stay.

"For a while during the past year or so I thought I would be going next time with the expectation of not returning," she wrote. But the Churches of Christ—her heart's labor—would be able to continue, "registered as they were from the beginning." As such, she wrote, "I plan to return, God willing."[7] She continued:

Two of the churches in Tokyo went together and entered the federation and others in other places may have done so. I do not know but none of the three churches in which I have served here in Shizuoka Prefecture have changed. Some one or two disbanded, thus forfeiting their right to continue as formerly. I fear in that case that a re-registration will be impossible. And to start a new work as we used to do may be impossible except as it may grow out of a present established work.[8]

Sarah finished the letter by promising to write again and to speak a lot when they were together again:

So you see from this that she whom you thought "dead yet speaketh." Ha. Yes, I am by God's grace (divine kindness) still living. In these trying times many have been the lessons impressed upon me and God's promises have been graciously verified. You in the homeland have received spiritual blessings no doubt, in your respective experiences and I hope to hear and be blessed from yours as well as mine.[9]

When the occupation army (fifteen hundred strong at Sarah's count) entered Sarah's city, her needs continued to be met.

"I soon gained twenty-five pounds," she later recalled. "They not only fed me, but gave me warm clothing and fuel . . . and rode me here and there in a jeep and gave me free transportation on the army trains to Tokyo."[10] Sarah was simply classified as recovered personnel.

It was a far cry from how she had previously been treated, and the townfolk took notice; it only added to her testimony. Sarah recalled:

When the Japanese saw the blessings that were being showered upon me, they exclaimed: "Surely the Supreme Being is with that woman!" To have these people recognize God and ascribe unto him the power for my deliverance made me rejoice that I had been counted worthy to suffer. Yes, God showed himself strong. He saved my life. He saved the property. But the victory of God's will as regards to his church in Japan is the source of greatest joy and thanksgiving. The religious law has been annulled. The union of church and state has been severed. Religious freedom is enjoyed. There is hope for the future. The Christians are not without vision, and the people in their dilemma are seeking truth.[11]

CHAPTER ELEVEN

Ardent Religious
Sentiment

O Lord, thou hast searched me, and known me.
Thou knowest my downsitting and mine uprising,
thou understandest my thought afar off.
Thou compassest my path and my lying down,
and art acquainted with all my ways.
For there is not a word in my tongue,
but, lo, O Lord, thou knowest it altogether.
Thou hast beset me behind and before,
and laid thine hand upon me.
Such knowledge is too wonderful for me;
it is high, I cannot attain unto it.
Whither shall I go from thy spirit?
or whither shall I flee from thy presence?

PSALM 139:1–7

*S*arah had waited long enough. It had been a month since she'd sent the letter to her sister Myrtle, but still no word back. This time, the missive went directly to Sarah's dear mother. On November 20, 1945, Sarah wrote a letter home:

> The Army Chaplain's Assistant will come by for this tomorrow morning, so I want to get it ready before going to bed. He gave me his name and address and says if you will address me in his care he will get your letter to me. . . . It seems strange that it is addressed to San Francisco, California, but that is the way all their mail comes, so please don't be afraid there is a mistake.[1]

The assistant told Sarah she should get an answer within twenty days, but that he might not be stationed in Shizuoka longer than a month. Sarah implored her mother to write immediately, having great hope that she might hear from her before Christmas.

Once the pleasantries were out of the way, there were tidbits of day-to-day life. Sarah had gone to Tokyo for a physical check-up, and joked that she had "killed two birds with one stone" by staying at the hospital while there. It was a Catholic hospital, and she had gone there on the advice on the American Embassy in Yokohama. She wrote:

> It is impossible for ordinary civies like myself to get hotel accommodations in Tokyo now, so I had a nice room with good care at the hospital. I enjoyed the food so much.[2]

She had a cold by the time she arrived, but her care kept it from getting worse. All the same, the doctor did tell her that heart was not very strong. "But I can make the trip home all right, he seems to think," she wrote. "Of course I can; I don't doubt that at all."[3]

The mornings were cold and frosty, and Sarah spent time outdoors readying wood for the coming winter. She had a tree cut down for burning, but it took longer than expected to cut it into pieces of the right length—especially since the days were so short. "I enjoy puttering around outside in the sunshine that is so warm and lovely these cool days," she wrote. "It is really more comfortable outside than it is in the house."[4] The woman and her daughter from Tokyo still stayed with Sarah, and she was grateful for the company. She was also grateful for the army food that was helping her return to her former weight.

"My scales need oil or repair perhaps so don't seem to be true," Sarah told her mother, "but my mirror tells the truth and I know I am gaining."[5]

Before the following summer, Sarah would be well enough to head home. And by then, her imprint on the city had been set. Sarah discovered that because so many believed her dead, there had been almost a total discontinuance of funds for her since 1943.[6] Not only that, but her accounts had been frozen. So great had been her impact on those around her, however, that in May 1946, the director of the Welfare Department of the Shizuoka Prefectural Government made an official recommendation that any money of hers that was being held be released. This was no friend or religious organization; it was a letter from the government of Japan regarding an American on its lands, less than a year after the bombings and surrender. The director wrote:

> Indeed, throughout the thirty years that she has been here, her career has been wholly devoted to social work, such as the preaching of the Gospel, managing of kindergarten, and relief of the sick and the helpless. She has often received insufficient funds for her work . . . while she herself has been living in

contented poverty, which fact is making a deep impression upon people about her.

Not only that, but there was more work in sight. Her latest plans, according to the recommendation, were to build a sanatorium for the weak once she returned to Japan. Her "ardent religious sentiment" was well-known, and the welfare department hoped that her wish would be "fulfilled soon for the good of Japan."[8]

By the time Sarah was ready to leave for home the following month, a group of prominent women from Shizuoka City had come to bid her farewell. They insisted, she wrote, that she return "as soon as possible and lead them into the way of truth." Her response? "The call comes ringing. The three churches are waiting."[9]

July 18, 1946, found Sarah in Texas, spending time with family after her long journey home. A letter went out to McCaleb and his second wife, Elizabeth, within a couple of months, full of apologies for not being in contact sooner. "The home-coming, with all that it has meant after almost seven years' absence, has resulted in a lot of talking to the neglect of writing," Sarah reported. "Then making my arrival in the heat of the summer made me lazy and slow." And that wasn't all. She had left her trusty Corona typewriter in Japan—having traded it for a kimono and sash—and a continuing tremor had become "such an affliction" that she could hardly write legibly with a pen. She found relief, however, with a portable Remington borrowed from a friend.[10]

It was a rich time with the relatives. Sarah's mother, who had not been well, immediately improved when her daughter arrived. Sarah's sister Nell came out from Birmingham and spent three weeks, and Sarah and her mother made plans to visit other family members in Tennessee, Alabama, and Florida, as soon as cooler weather arrived and they were both physically fit for the trip. "Although I eat and sleep well, I haven't gained any weight," she reported. "But I tell them I am no doubt of the lean kind and it's the lean horse for the long race."[11]

The problem wasn't just her weight. Years of malnutrition and stress had left her teeth, hair, and eyes a mess. Much would need to be done before she could return to her beloved Japan. Other missionaries, stateside since the early days of the war, were anxious to go back, too. Sarah believed, however, that it was still too early for that to happen. She wrote to the McCalebs:

> Even the big denominations have not succeeded in getting passports for those whom they have chosen to send and for whom housing and food is guaranteed by their several representatives over there. My opinion is that it is a bit early for missionaries to go. There is not only the housing, food, and fuel situation to face but there is no money exchange yet. Folks can't get by without a little money anyway. Living is sky high over there . . . and the world situation is very unsettled. The people in Japan are unsettled. At present it is a real scramble for food.[12]

In addition, Sarah had been told that the occupational army would not permit missionaries to give anything—not even a book—to the Japanese. She did learn, however, that the postal service would soon accept packages to be sent overseas, and planned to gather one together for her faithful friend Iki-San before long.

Sarah had also learned that two of the churches she had been associated with were still meeting regularly: one in Shizuoka and the other at Okitsu. Not so of the other two; the congregation at

Shimizu had not recovered from the burning of its chapel, and things were bleak for those in Mazawa. Sarah could only hope and pray. With the help of the workers at Okitsu, she believed the church would be all right—as long as neither the government nor the still-present federation of churches stepped in to close it. She wrote:

> It remains to be seen whether independents will retain their full and free independence. I heard before I left that all work already established would be left but any new work must be done in connection with, and out from, any churches already established. No worker native or foreign can go out and start a work independent of others. Now that we have only four or five churches left, their responsibility is big in case this rule is put into operation. After all, is not this the scriptural method of growth?[13]

Sarah would not write the McCalebs again for five months; her days instead were filled with the aforementioned visits to family in various states, as well as seemingly endless dental work. It was "mostly extractions," she wrote, "and you know what an ordeal that is." The dentist was going slow on account of her debilitated condition.[14]

Sarah and her mother were enjoying their travels, but truth be told, Sarah's heart remained in Japan. She hoped she wouldn't have to wait any later than the beginning of 1948 for the government to once again be willing to issue passports to missionaries. Some, however, had been able to make it back, mostly using creative strategies. Harry Robert Fox Sr., for example, traveled to Nagasaki in September 1945. He worked as an interpreter investigating casualties from the atomic bomb, and took advantage of the opportunity to check out church progress for the folks back home. He and O. D. Bixler began recruiting missionaries to join them in Japan, and they returned with twenty of them in tow. They brought a boatload of goats and cows, as well, hoping to help set the hungry nation back on its feet. E. A. Rhodes was also about to return, thanks to the fact that he was a dependent of his army son, based in Yokohama.[15]

While there, Bixler took a weekend trip to Shizuoka, and reported to Sarah that levels of interest were high, and that he considered possibilities for her further work there unlimited. "This is of course encouraging and I am thankful the work moves forward," she wrote the McCalebs.[16]

If only she could keep up with it.

CHAPTER TWELVE

Comforting with the Same Comfort

Blessed are the poor in spirit: for theirs is the kingdom of heaven.
Blessed are they that mourn: for they shall be comforted.
Blessed are the meek: for they shall inherit the earth.
Blessed are they which do hunger and thirst
after righteousness: for they shall be filled.
Blessed are the merciful: for they shall obtain mercy.
Blessed are the pure in heart: for they shall see God.
Blessed are the peacemakers: for they
shall be called the children of God.
Blessed are they which are persecuted for righteousness' sake:
for theirs is the kingdom of heaven.
Blessed are ye, when men shall revile you,
and persecute you, and shall say all manner of evil
against you falsely, for my sake.
Rejoice, and be exceeding glad: for great is
your reward in heaven: for so persecuted they
the prophets which were before you.

MATTHEW 5:3–12

*T*hroughout Sarah's missionary life, she had a great friend and supporter in I. B. Bradley. Long acting as treasurer for Sarah's funds, he was a constant and consistent link to home. But by 1947, due to declining health, he asked to be relieved of the task. Sarah fondly recalled his faithful service:

> From the time I first talked of going to Japan, in 1915, Brother Bradley, who was then preaching for the church at Dickson, my home congregation, very graciously assumed this responsibility. During all those years before the war, he forwarded funds each month that would come from interested friends or congregations. Words cannot express my heartfelt thanks and appreciation to Brother and Sister Bradley for this faithful fellowship through the years. God knows, and God will reward.[1]

Others in her congregation agreed to take over the work, but truth be told, there wasn't that much to pick up. In February of 1947, Sarah reported that there was only one regular contributor left, a woman who gave about ten dollars per year.[2]

Sarah, however, was still not one to be daunted. Later that year, after the visits with family, she was off to Los Angeles to prepare written materials for her friends overseas. Many were interested in her return to Japan, but Sister Andrews, according to *Gospel Advocate*, was "probably more interested than anyone else."[3]

"Friends are also asking if I expect to return to Japan, and I rejoice to reply that I am preparing to return," she wrote in November 1947. "I take great delight in feeling that I am even now in service for the Japanese in my efforts to prepare Bible-study helps for them while here having access to good libraries."[4] The word from Japan was indeed promising; according to Sarah, "As soon as the dark curtain of war lifted and religious freedom was granted, there followed a revival of interest in the Christian religion among the Japanese such as had never been witnessed before."[5]

Just before and just after the war, she wrote, the outlook for the Church of Christ in Japan was indeed bleak. She now had great hope, however:

> But now the prospects were never brighter. Before returning home last year I rented my home in Shizuoka to a Christian couple who are conducting a private school there with great success. It is a sewing school, but English; and, of course, Bible and other subjects are taught. From the start there has been a capacity enrollment of some two hundred fifty students.[6]

The biggest challenge, however, was that due to a lack of accommodations and supplies, additional students weren't admitted. Sarah put out the word that the school was in dire need of sewing machines, and asked anyone who would be willing to donate one to contact her directly.

"Many people are being introduced to the church through the school," she told the readers of *Gospel Advocate*, and there were reports that attendance at church was increasing, too. "Many also attend the Bible classes, and several have asked to be baptized." A certain Brother Okada was preaching at the churches in both Shizuoka and Okitsu, and was "loved and respected by all."[7] She continued:

> I hear from the Japanese Christians frequently, and they write encouragingly as follows: "Democratic Japan is open to Christianity. . . . The newly appointed Premier is a believer in Christ. . . . The people of Japan, even among the intelligentsia, are hungry for

spiritual food; Christianity just fills this need. . . . The work in the
church and school is full of promising aspects. . . . All the students
are looking forward to your coming next year. . . . Many people
will be at the station to meet you. . . . We are praying for your health
and for your return. . . Opportunities are limitless. . . . You have a
big job here in Shizuoka." Of course I am eager to return.[8]

She was eager to begin a new work there, too. As the Shizuoka
government had said in its recommendation, Sarah hoped to
open a rest home in the hills, convenient to the three congregations in her section of the country. She wrote of these plans in
Gospel Advocate:

> The home will be primarily for convalescents who can be taught
> the truth and encouraged to take it to their family and friends
> along with some rules of health when they return home. The
> minister of the Welfare Department in Shizuoka Prefecture
> pleads that I return and carry out this plan, saying he will assist
> in making it a reality. The Japanese Christians are interested in
> this project, and I feel that I can do my best service in that line
> of work.[9]

After all, she could certainly relate. "I have been frail so long, and
delight in 'comforting them with the same comfort wherewith I am
comforted of God,'" she continued. "Jesus, the great lover of the
souls of men, did not neglect the social welfare of those for whom
he gave himself. He frequently paved the way into the soul by
helping the body." Words couldn't express the level of need for such
a work in Japan, according to Sarah, "where sick and well are
crowded together in a disastrous condition to both."[10]

The immediate plans were to start small with a building of simple
construction. But she hoped to eventually have enough land for the

gardening of fruits, berries, and vegetables, as well as room for chickens, bees, goats, and maybe a cow. She wrote:

> These will provide some maintenance for the home and give some diversional activities and entertainment to the patients. It has been said: "Who loves a garden, still his Eden keeps." Jesus loved the flowers, flocks, mountains, the sea, the sky. When God created the world, he placed man in a garden. Would not our Father have the world a glorious garden?[11]

But the gardens and the property wouldn't be just for those who stayed there. Once a month, Sarah wrote, she would like to have a time at the home for visitors to spend the day there. "Such Christian atmosphere which we hope will be maintained in the home shall surely be conducive to spiritual as well as physical health." Financial gifts would be helpful in bringing the vision to reality, Sarah continued:

> But, as in the past, I shall proceed in accordance with the amount entrusted to me. I have thought of selling my home in Shizuoka and using the proceeds in establishing this rest home; but I trust this will not be necessary, since the property in Shizuoka City is so essential to the Lord's work there.[12]

No doubt, Sarah's visions and plans challenged those still in the States. But if there had ever been a time for such a bold venture, it was then. Sarah believed in the importance of Japan's influence in the world, and wrote:

> For a century Japan has been the foremost nation in the Orient. The aspiration that led to the war was to form a "Greater East Asia," it being the big brother; but it failed. This dream was wordly, without God. Defeated Japan still has the talent for leadership,

however, and we should help it to the point where it can use it for good to its neighbors. To give Japan the Gospel is the answer to its greatest need and service to others.[13]

The following months were filled with prayers, plans, and preparation. Spring 1948 found Sarah still in Los Angeles, still toiling away at the series of Bible studies to be used by the Japanese. "I am making the outlines rather full; hence, it takes much time," she reported to the readers of *Gospel Advocate*. "At any rate, I am trying to do my humble bit toward helping the Japanese to a proper understanding of the Bible. They need guidance."[14]

Sarah had continued to be in touch with her Japanese brethren, and wrote that she had received several recent letters with good reports:

An air-mail letter received Saturday states that there were one hundred twenty children in Bible study at the Shizuoka church Sunday morning, March 28, and the attendance at worship was fine. They add that a prayer for my speedy return is offered each Lord's day. The work at Okitsu, sixteen miles from Shizuoka, is also encouraging.[15]

Not so much so in Shimizu, where the meeting place had yet to be rebuilt since the bombings. The members gathered in a home, "but it seems inadequate," Sarah continued. "I hope and pray to rebuild there sometime, so that the work may be revived and new opportunities grasped. It will take perhaps $1,000 to rebuild even a very modest house."[16]

As anxious as she was to return, there was suddenly other business to attend to—and heartbreaking business at that. On May 10, 1948, Sarah's mother, Ada, died in Florida. According to the obituary, all nine of Ada's children attended the service, as well as a handful of grandsons who served as pallbearers. The legacy of Christian character was felt throughout; in addition to godly works by her immediate relatives, the church that she and her late husband helped found all those years before had grown to twelve hundred members.

One final time, the example she set for Sarah and others was on display, and a favorite poem, "My Bible and I," written by M. H. Knobloch, was read at the service:

We've traveled together, my Bible and I,
Through all kinds of weather, with smile, or with sigh,
In sorrow or sunshine, in tempest or calm;
Thy friendship unchanging, my lamp and my psalm.

We've traveled together, my Bible and I,
When life had grown weary, and death even was nigh,
But all through the darkness of mist or of wrong,
I found Thee a solace, a prayer or a song.

So who shall part us, my Bible and I?
Shall errors or follies, or New-lights who try?
Shall shadow or substance, or stone for good bread,
Supplant Thy sound wisdom, give folly instead?

Oh, no my dear Bible, exponent of light!
Thou sword of the Spirit, put error to flight;
And still through life's journey until my last sigh,
We'll travel together, my Bible and I.[17]

CHAPTER THIRTEEN

A Veritable Ingrate

And though the Lord give you the bread
of adversity, and the water of affliction,
yet shall not thy teachers be removed
into a corner any more, but thine eyes
shall see thy teachers: And thine ears shall hear
a word behind thee, saying, This is the way,
walk ye in it, when ye turn to the right hand,
and when ye turn to the left.

ISAIAH 30:20–21

wo weeks after Ada's death, Sarah admitted that she hadn't been able to "throw off" the sorrow. "We miss Mother sorely and shall continue to miss her, but I know we must remember that our loss is her gain," she wrote the McCalebs. "No doubt she is at rest in peace. We children have much to be thankful for and many rich and sweet memories to cherish."[1]

Even though Ada had died in Florida, it made the most sense to bring her back to Dickson, where so much of the family's Christian heritage began. I. B. Bradley preached the sermon, and "several spoke of how sweet and beautiful it all was," Sarah wrote. There were almost one hundred flower arrangements from family and friends, and the Dickson undertaker said he had never seen so many out-of-town floral offerings before. "Mother was indeed a rare and beautiful character and everybody's friend."[2]

Ada had suffered much in the last months of her life, brought on by a weakened heart, hardened arteries, and bad circulation. At the end, though, she "just peacefully slept away." Sarah hadn't only been concerned with her mother's health; there was still more dental work to be done for herself, and after returning to Florida with family members, she settled herself in for the ordeal.[3]

By mid-July, Sarah boasted a whole new set of upper teeth, and wrote the McCalebs that she was adjusting well to them. The dentist told her, however, that she would have to wait on the lower set until she had gotten stronger. He agreed to patch them so they'd last a little longer. Sarah wrote to the McCalebs about the long procedure:

> This dental work has taken a lot of time. The dentist is in Lakeland, fourteen miles from Bartow, and I have been going most of the time by bus. Bess insists that she take me, but she is not strong and has home duties and the weather has been pretty warm, so I don't let her worry to drive me over there.

> Guess you are wondering what has become of me. Or you may have decided that I am a veritable ingrate. [Depending on the time of her appointment, the trip to Lakeland and back could take all day. Add to that the fact that there was plenty of company to attend

to, many friends to see, and meetings at church and neighboring congregations. It was no wonder that it had been almost eight weeks since her last letter.] I regret my failure to write you sooner and want to assure you that it hasn't been because I've forgotten you nor because I'm unmindful of all your kindnesses to me. I think of you every day and always with gratitude for your friendship and interest.[4]

There was something else she was thankful for, too; the McCalebs, who were still in Los Angeles, were keeping up with all of Sarah's self-proclaimed "junk" while she traveled the rest of the country. "Hope my stuff is not too much in your way," she wrote. "I surely appreciate your taking care of it for me. Hope I can do something for you sometime."[5]

Sarah made the rounds from Florida to see other family members in Tennessee and Texas, and they all begged her once again to stay in the States. Regardless, she headed to California in January 1949 with her mind set on the sea. "I've had a very pleasant holiday season with loved ones here," she wrote, "but I know I mustn't tarry longer. March isn't far off now, and I have much to do before leaving for Japan again."[6]

The next time the McCalebs received a letter from Sarah, it was from her cabin on the SS *Flying Scud*. She had just had supper as well as "a little ozone on deck," and was ready to recount her experiences since seeing them last. The main feat to report was that she'd finally learned how to eat with her new teeth. She wrote on May 18, 1949:

It has indeed been an ordeal and I've lost weight in the effort, but believe the worst is over and am thankful. The dentist gave me instructions as to how to adjust them myself, and I went to a 10-cent store in San Francisco and got a supply of sand paper and a little knife and have whittled and sand-papered to beat the band.[7]

Impressions were taken for the new teeth only a week after the last four had been extracted, she said, and then the new plate was put in two days after that. And that day was the day before she left Los Angeles with the plate in her pocket. "Ha! I positively could not use them either for eating or talking," she wrote. "Am getting on fine now and hope as the days come and go I'll get so accustomed to them that they will be a part of me."[8]

The trip had been an adventurous one. It started with the journey from California up to Seattle; due to rough waters, the boat arrived too late for anyone to disembark. The next morning, however, Sarah had grabbed her suitcase, headed for town, and made requests about a missionary room being vacant. One room was, and since the next boat wouldn't leave Seattle for several days, she had "a nice long stay there, and really enjoyed it."[9]

The boat was set to leave at midnight, but she boarded in time for supper and went to bed early. She awoke, though, "when the old *Scud* weighed anchor and crept out through Puget Sound." Sailing was smooth all the way to Adak, Alaska, she wrote, and she even got to see a whale spouting water. The next whale in sight, a couple of days later, wasn't nearly so inspiring; it was dead, "and oh how he did smell." As for Adak, it was mostly a frozen mass akin to the ice cream Sarah had been served on the ship. "The mountains were beautiful with snow almost to the water's edge, but it was quite a desolate-looking place, and I was glad to stay in my warm room on the boat," she recalled.[10]

Things were much different this time around. Sarah was no longer a young girl off for unknown adventure, nor a woman returning on the verge of World War II. By now, she was a seasoned missionary of fifty-six, one who had seen torture, adversity, and loss even in the midst of victories. Sarah had never lost her resolve. And every so often, the God she loved would reward her for it—in both large and small ways.

"I have a room all to myself," she wrote. "There are two beds in the room, but since there are only six passengers aboard and there are accommodations for eight, there was no one assigned to occupy the room with me and I am glad. I occupy either bed. When I get tired of one, I crawl into the other." It was, she recalled, one of the nicest staterooms she had had on a voyage, complete with a private bathroom and shower, a desk with good light, a chest of drawers, lots of storage space under each bunk, and two closets. Two "mascots" (a couple of girls ages two and four who were the children of Presbyterian missionaries) and another woman, a San Francisco lady going to visit her daughter-in-law in Tokyo, rounded out the set. The food was good, she reported, but she spent two days of the voyage in bed with a headache. "The captain and everybody were worried about me, but I told them I'd be OK, and was as usual," she wrote. It was a little different than the migraines that had plagued her in the past.[11]

By May 20, 1949, the SS *Flying Scud* had arrived in Yokohama, and due to a downpour of rain, it took several days to get all of Sarah's belongings off of the boat and through customs. But what a party was there to meet her! There was Iki-San with the man she had married, Brother Okada, and several other Americans and Japanese whose lives she had touched. "In all there were fourteen standing [and] waving as the *Scud* drew up to the pier," she wrote. "How happy I was to see them all and to set foot once more on terra firma." And the welcomes kept coming. After visiting with friends in Yokohama, Sarah boarded the train for her home. Iki-San, who had gone on ahead, met her at the Numazu station with her two sons, "and we had a nice visit while the train stood there for five minutes." Then, when the train passed Okitsu, even though it didn't make a stop, "a large group of friends were standing in front of the meeting house, waiting." And at Shizuoka, her final destination, "there were some fifty at the station to meet me," she recalled. "Newspaper agents were taking pictures and one of the brethren took moving pictures of me as I got off the train and greeted the crowd who had come to welcome me. There were write-ups in several Japanese papers. Of course the military personnel on the train were interested in the reception I was getting all along the way." Since arriving in Shizuoka, she wrote, she had had many additional callers, and sixty-five people from the area churches gathered for a welcome-home celebration. "I was so happy to be safely back again that I could hardly keep still."[12]

Things were definitely looking up. There was even the promise of regular food. Sarah was eligible for groceries from the Overseas Supply Service for non-military personnel—even if there was a catch. "This marketing must be done by the individual holding the permit, so that means I must go one hundred miles to market," she wrote. "Ha. The prices are a bit higher than in the States, but it is American groceries." A group of church ladies from Los Angeles had agreed to send her a package of food once a month, "which will help out greatly, I am sure, and save me those long, trying trips to Tokyo on the train," she said. "Of course I don't eat much and will not need a great deal."[13]

By now, she was well accustomed to overcoming hurdles.

CHAPTER FOURTEEN

Back at the Post of Duty

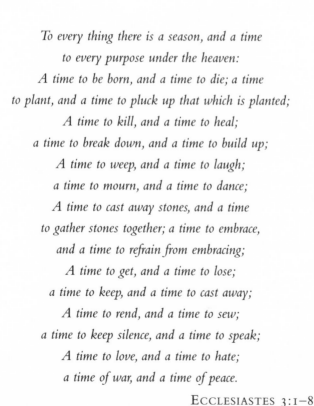

To every thing there is a season, and a time
to every purpose under the heaven:
A time to be born, and a time to die; a time
to plant, and a time to pluck up that which is planted;
A time to kill, and a time to heal;
a time to break down, and a time to build up;
A time to weep, and a time to laugh;
a time to mourn, and a time to dance;
A time to cast away stones, and a time
to gather stones together; a time to embrace,
and a time to refrain from embracing;
A time to get, and a time to lose;
a time to keep, and a time to cast away;
A time to rend, and a time to sew;
a time to keep silence, and a time to speak;
A time to love, and a time to hate;
a time of war, and a time of peace.

ECCLESIASTES 3:1–8

*W*ithin a month, the reality of living back in Shizuoka had set in—and that reality was not so cheery. The rainy season had begun, and with it, Sarah's health had taken another turn. In a letter to the McCalebs, Sarah admitted:

> Fatigue, exposure to the cold in the Klondikes, and perhaps improper eating on the boat threw me into a spell with my kidneys and bladder by the time I reached Yokohama. Having all my teeth pulled in such a short time before leaving the States may have had something to do with bringing on the trouble. At any rate, the condition worsened after I got here, so I went to a doctor in Tokyo. . . . I got relief in a few days and came back home, but still have to be careful not to overdo, nor get chilled. I'll probably have to be careful all during the rainy season which lasts until the middle of July. The weather is damp and cool now, but when the rains cease it'll get hot and steamy.[1]

In addition to the missionary work—and the steady stream of callers—Sarah had much to do in terms of getting her house back in order. When she left Los Angeles, she carried twenty-six pieces of baggage and freight with her, all of which she had packed and crated herself. Out of those, two had been lost: a steamer trunk and a wooden box. Sarah traveled back to Yokohama and spent almost three hours at the customs pier in search of the missing items, but to no avail. "I've submitted a claims letter giving a value of two hundred fifty dollars for these two pieces of freight," she wrote, "but I'd rather have the trunk and box intact than the money." They were full of gifts from the California church members for Sarah to give to the Japanese.[2]

The folks back home had indeed been generous. A women's magazine based in Austin had taken up a collection of items for the rest home, and the supplies included towels, bed linens, quilts, and table linens. There was also enough money to purchase a refrigerator and stove, which Sarah had picked up in San Francisco to be loaded directly onto the boat.[3]

Sarah still had plenty to unpack, but she didn't want to go too far before painting the woodwork in her kitchen. "I had to use wood in an open fire box with no outlet for smoke during the war," she wrote. "So this house is a smoked-up-smoke-house. The black must be removed before painting, so we're using lye, and it is really hard work." She had the help of some Japanese girls, as well as the Sugiyamas, a Christian family who stayed at the house in her absence. "They took care of the place nicely while I was gone and did much repair work," she continued. "It surely is nice to be home again and back at my post of duty."[4]

The days passed and the work continued. Sarah, however, still challenged by her health, began requesting that the letters sent from the States be sent by regular mail rather than military channels, so they'd arrive directly at her door. "It'll save me the long walk to the APO post office (*sic*) in town every day," she wrote the McCalebs. "I already see that I'm going to be really busy and must conserve both time and strength. . . . I know you will understand."[5]

Her request turned out to be prophetic. By the following spring, Sarah came down with a case of pneumonia severe enough that it left her with a weakened heart. "With opportunities so great here now, it is hard to apply the reins on myself," she admitted the next summer. "I'm hoping and praying that reinforcements may come to this field ere long. The task is far too great for me." Besides, she continued, her years of service were dwindling. "Two couples from the homeland are really needed here and the sooner the better. I am thinking I'll appeal through the papers, or maybe just write a few friends about the urgency of the need. . . . I believe the Lord of the harvest will send someone and will continue to pray."[6]

In the meantime, Sarah was doing her best to take care of herself. After closing the Bible classes for the summer, she and a friend went to a hot spring on the Idzu Peninsula, treating themselves to a Japanese hotel for a few days. "I really rested there and enjoyed it and felt much better when I got home," Sarah wrote. While in the mountains, she and the friend visited a member of the church who lived nearby, and that woman and her mother took them all to another hotel on the beach for a night. "The hotel was in a very lovely spot overlooking the beach," Sarah recalled. "The waves were so high that night that the other members of the party could not sleep for the roar, but as usual I slept well." The church member requested some evangelistic work in the area, and Sarah made plans to return with a couple of preachers and Iki-San, still her faithful friend. "The inhabitants of that village know nothing of Christianity," she wrote. "I'd like to get some literature ready to give out when we go, if this heat wave breaks. Can't hope to do much as long as the weather is so warm. It is usually midnight before I can get to sleep, and then I perspire so throughout the night that I wake tired the next morning, and so the days pass."[7]

Back in the States, Sarah's family was dealing with challenges of its own—and the news finally reached foreign shores. Sarah's older brother Bernard Binga "Pete" Andrews—the last of the siblings still living in Dickson, had passed away, and she was the only sibling that couldn't make it to the funeral. "The family sent me a cablegram which came as a great shock and grief," she told the McCalebs. The cause was a blood clot, and "he had not passed his sixty-first birthday," Sarah wrote. I. B. Bradley preached at the funeral, just as he had done for Sarah's mother, and since she couldn't be there, Sarah's Japanese friends held a memorial service in his honor. "The Japanese here are so kind and considerate of me in this sorrow," she continued. "I appreciate all but can't seem to overcome the cloud of grief."[8]

Sarah found some joy, however, in the fact that the workers had found a "nice location for the Shimizu work"—as well as the small fact that blackberries were in season. "I've never enjoyed the black-berries here like I have this year," she wrote. "Am still hopeful that I can transplant the vines to the rest home in the country. However, I realize I can't leave here until someone comes to relieve me. I am not trying to find a location for the rest home until a prospect for reinforcements comes."[9]

Those reinforcements were not quick in coming at all. The years passed, and Sarah continued to soldier on. "This is work in hard places," she admitted in a letter written just before Christmas 1953. "But God's grace is ever sufficient. There is eternal purpose in this service that gives inward courage and joy even when outward results appear discouraging and sometimes grievous."[10]

The good news was that the churches Sarah had been a part of had continued to grow in both faith and works, even if not as fast as she would have liked. The Sugiyama family, who had lived with Sarah in Shizuoka for several years, had built a sewing school about twenty miles away, and it had come complete with living quarters. Thus, they would be moving out, and a widowed friend and her two daughters would be moving in to act as caretakers of the chapel connected to Sarah's still-standing Sears, Roebuck, and Co. house. Because of fire hazards, she explained, it was a Japanese custom to never leave a building vacant.[11]

As for the rest house in Numazu, it was almost complete. All it lacked at the time of Sarah's letter was a working well for water. "When I was there a few days ago the pump was drilling away, but it seemed quite a feat," she wrote. "You may be interested to know that this is to be an artesian well, and the water is from an underground river which has its source in the foothills of Mt. Fuji. The water is very pure as well as cold." It was so cold, in fact, that there were reportedly no fish at the place where the stream flowed into the ocean. Once the house was complete, a Numazu evangelist and his family of five would move in temporarily, and it would be a great improvement over their previous home, "a small room over a fish shop," Sarah explained. "It'll be rather crowded in the new house with eight of us there. . . . I do hope and pray that all of us together can do much service for Christ in that locality." Sarah believed that within the next few months, she'd be settled in. "This will probably be my permanent address until my sojourn on earth is finished," she wrote. "None of us know how long that will be, but I'm thankful to say that I've felt better than usual the past few months."[12]   No doubt, the promise of the next adventure had buoyed her spirits.

CHAPTER FIFTEEN

Weakness and Strength

And, behold, I am with thee, and will keep thee
in all places whither thou goest,
and will bring thee again into this land;
for I will not leave thee, until I have done that
which I have spoken to thee of.

GENESIS 28:15

Though Sarah continued to be a visionary and self-determined force, she was fully aware that she couldn't do it all alone. When it came time for preaching at the newly opened rest home, she called on an old family friend: Harry Robert Fox Jr., whom she had known since he had been a boy. Fox had first traveled to Japan in the late 1920s with his parents, staying until 1935 when Harry Robert Fox Sr. needed medical treatment back in the States.[1]

Not only had young Fox fondly remembered the attention Sarah had given him and his siblings when she visited their home in Tanakura—a major event since they lived so far off the beaten path—but he also recalled living in her Shizuoka house while she took a furlough to the U.S. This time around, he would encounter her as an adult and a fired-up missionary. Fox and his wife had come back to Japan in 1947, a short time after Fox's father had returned. He and a group of others founded Ibaraki Christian College and ended up staying for eleven years.[2]

Before he arrived back in Japan, however, Fox Jr. had been stirred up by a series of preachers who had opened his eyes to the possibility of a Christian life based on a personal relationship with God, rather than simply rules and straight-laced regulations. It changed his heart, it changed his motivation, and ultimately, it changed the way he perceived the work of the missionaries he knew in Japan. He was all too happy to help. He welcomed the invitation to speak at the rest home as well as the congregation in Shizuoka, and spent endless hours poring over church-related matters with the woman who considered him like a nephew.[3]

She had long told him about her hopes of raising the money, buying the lot, and erecting the building. She wanted it to be large enough for a church auditorium downstairs as well as living quarters upstairs, plus extra rooms where older members of the church could live in their latter years. All that happened as planned, but when Fox finally saw it, he was surprised. "She said that after the building was built, it was larger and more luxurious than she had anticipated and that she felt embarrassed to be living in it," he recalled. "In my estimation, however, it appeared to be a very modest structure."[4]

It was simply bigger than her hard-won humility would allow.

Sarah moved from Shizuoka to Numazu in June 1954, but she was far from willing to let go of the efforts near her previous home. It was a difficult time. Sarah wrote of "turmoils in Shizuoka" that delayed her "in every way and upset me physically." In addition to the contentions between missionaries that challenged the levels of traditionalism in the work, there was the recent American hydrogen bomb testing on Bikini Atoll to contend with, and the fact that some Japanese fishermen from the Shizuoka Prefecture had developed radiation sickness from the experiment's fallout. (The boat's radio telegraph operator actually died.)[5]

"I realize that I shouldn't have permitted myself to suffer physically as I did," she wrote. "But sometimes it seems altho' the spirit is willing, the flesh is weak!" She had been eager to continue her Bible class work at Shizuoka and Shimizu but finally "had a physical break." "I feel some better since moving to Numazu . . . but still have to go slow." She decided not to teach again until the fall.[6]

Even then, however, she remained a self-proclaimed "slow-go." "I don't seem to get even half of the things done I plan to do," she wrote Fox's wife, Gerry, in October 1954. Other brothers in the faith had planned trips to help her out, and she was looking forward to their visits. The Foxes invited Sarah out to the college at Ibaraki, as well, but there was news from home, so she dared not venture far: her sister in Birmingham, Alabama, was seriously ill.[7]

And it wouldn't be long before she was seriously ill herself. In a letter to the Foxes dated November 1955, she admitted she was sitting up in bed with a typewriter on her lap for the first time in three weeks. Another letter, dated a month later, said, "I regret that I cannot give you a first-hand report on recent happenings of the work at the four stations." She had been too sick. A high fever had left her so weak and emaciated that she hadn't been able to take the train, even though she'd had "encouraging reports" about the work that had gone on without her. "The work at Numazu continues to grow," she continued. "There was another baptism last week and the meetings are well attended." Besides that, there would soon be a Christian wedding, the first to be held there. "The neighbors are all excited over this Christian wedding," she wrote. "I imagine a crowd will gather along the street to see the bridal party arrive. I had feared the children would come peeping in at the windows since there is no fence to bar them out." Happily, however, the company that built the house agreed to hurriedly build a fence before the wedding would take place. "The workmen are busy accomplishing this purpose and we are all rejoicing," she said. "The weather is balmy and beautiful. I have always enjoyed the falls in Japan."[8]

Before long, at least one of Sarah's illnesses had a name—and not a good one. After a thorough examination, she later reported, the doctors found her trouble to be "a chronic colitis and a marked enteroptosis." The worst of it was that they had ordered her to travel back to the States to find a proper girdle for holding her intestines in place. The doctor tried to have her fitted by a company in Tokyo, but to no avail. "The man came to Yokohama and took my measurements and then again to fit the girdle, but Dr. J. was not satisfied with the make . . . they put a kind of elastic binding on me and let me come home."[9]

The overseas voyage would end up being her last trip home, a furlough that would last for two years. Family and friends pleaded with her not to return to Japan, but in July 1958 she boarded a boat regardless. There was still work to be done. Sarah, now age sixty-five, told of the voyage in a letter to her friends:

> Had a rather rough voyage, but since I am a good sailor, I got on fine. The only diversions on the turbulent waters during the two weeks of sailing were the sight of another boat in the distance and a whale spouting water high into the air not far from the boat. We passed through a storm soon after leaving the American coast and ran into a typhoon shortly before reaching Yokohama. I stayed in bed during those upheavals and had a good rest, leaving the termination of the storms with God.[10]

By comparison to the rest of the life that Sarah had lived, a storm at sea was a relatively small event.

As usual, she received a hero's welcome, with Iki-San and other friends surprising her; they had taken the journey to meet her so they could all ride the train back to Numazu together. "How happy I was to see them all!" she recalled. Another group met the train in Numazu, then they headed for church and a celebratory meal.[11]

"In the days following I was busy with many things, and had company galore," she wrote. "I had to take things as slowly as possible. But there were some things that had to have prompt attention, among which was a trip to Shizuoka to have my dollars changed to yen." Then there were more welcome meetings to attend, and reports of the work moving forward. But once again, it was not as quickly as Sarah would have liked. "The faith of some of the members has grown cold," she wrote, "and we hope they can be encouraged to return to the fold. One of the meeting houses is in dire need of repair, and the church at Shimizu, which has been worshipping in a home, needs a larger meeting place, and I want to help them a little later on, God willing." In addition, there were plans for meetings at Numazu and Okitsu during the fall.[12]

This time, however, the work would not be Sarah's to complete. The coming years would be a continuous downhill slide of her health. The letters became more and more infrequent, the bedstays longer and more serious. In addition to the problems with her intestines, Sarah had tuberculosis, and as she aged, doctors said her heart was representative of one twenty years her senior. The climate, the stress, and the delicate constitution she'd had since her youth had finally caught up with her, and in 1961 a series of strokes brought her to her final days. Her beloved Japanese friends tended to her day and night, hating to see her suffer. But over and over, as the story has long been told, she repeated a favorite Scripture, Psalm 103, to the point that all her weak body could do was mouth the words.

> Bless the Lord, O my soul: and all that is within me, bless his holy name.
> Bless the Lord, O my soul, and forget not all his benefits:
> Who forgiveth all thine iniquities; who healeth all thy diseases;
> Who redeemeth thy life from destruction; who crowneth thee with lovingkindness and tender mercies;
> Who satisfieth thy mouth with good things; so that thy youth is renewed like the eagle's.
> The Lord executeth righteousness and judgment for all that are oppressed.
> He made known his ways unto Moses, his acts unto the children of Israel.
> The Lord is merciful and gracious, slow to anger, and plenteous in mercy.
> He will not always chide: neither will he keep his anger for ever.
> He hath not dealt with us after our sins; nor rewarded us according to our iniquities.

For as the heaven is high above the earth, so great is his mercy
toward them that fear him.

As far as the east is from the west, so far hath he removed our
transgressions from us.

Like as a father pitieth his children, so the Lord pitieth them
that fear him.

For he knoweth our frame; he remembereth that we are dust.

As for man, his days are as grass: as a flower of the field, so
he flourisheth.

For the wind passeth over it, and it is gone; and the place
thereof shall know it no more.

But the mercy of the Lord is from everlasting to everlasting
upon them that fear him, and his righteousness unto
children's children;

To such as keep his covenant, and to those that remember his
commandments to do them.

The Lord hath prepared his throne in the heavens; and his
kingdom ruleth over all.

Bless the Lord, ye his angels, that excel in strength, that do his
commandments, hearkening unto the voice of his word.

Bless ye the Lord, all ye his hosts; ye ministers of his, that do
his pleasure.

Bless the Lord, all his works in all places of his dominion: bless
the Lord, O my soul.

Finally, on September 16, 1961, her sufferings, her challenges, and
her physical limitations came to an end. Surrounded by friends, she
passed from this life to the next. Such was her influence that twenty
years after her death, in 1981, one hundred Japanese attended a
memorial service marking the anniversary. Many still admit that
missions work in Japan is a challenging, often discouraging task. It is
no quick work, no simple conversion, but instead requires a faithful,
steady hand and large doses of optimism.

Sarah Andrews, slight, sickly, and female though she was, had managed to take on an entire nation with humility, faith, and simple dependence on God. On Sarah's death, *Gospel Advocate* reported:

> We who live in the plenty and often luxury of the United States, among friends and family satisfactions, are incapable of understanding the real price which missionaries pay when they leave all these and go to faraway places to spend their lives in mission work.

Her entire life, with little exception, had been spent in and near Shizuoka, the magazine continued, and she had been a noble woman indeed. "Her body has been placed in the soil of the people she loved and served, and her life is enshrined in her affections. How better could any life end?"[13]

EPILOGUE

Preparing the Way

Therefore are they before the throne of God,
and serve him day and night in his temple:
and he that sitteth on the throne shall dwell among them.
They shall hunger no more, neither thirst any more;
neither shall the sun light on them, nor any heat.
For the Lamb which is in the midst of the throne
shall feed them, and shall lead them unto
living fountains of waters: and God
shall wipe away all tears from their eyes.

REVELATION 7:15–17

*A*sk anyone who knew Sarah Sheppard Andrews what she was like, and you'll most likely hear the same handful of words: determined. devoted. And all the same, frail. Family and friends recall her reading her Bible in Japanese even while in the States; being desperate to return to her beloved missions work despite the fact her health worried virtually everyone around her; and being headstrong about the amount of work yet to be done.

One family member, however, was able to add a different set of memories than the rest. Wanda Stuart, niece of T. B. and Myrtle Thompson, had moved to Japan with her air force husband earlier that year; she was chosen to represent Sarah's relatives at the funeral. After arriving in Numazu by train, Wanda and her travel companions were greeted with several men holding large banners with Sarah's name on them. The men led them to taxis that took them to Sarah's home, where they met with more than a dozen missionaries. The Bixlers and Hettie Lee Ewing were among them.[1]

"I don't know what I'd have done without Hettie Lee sitting behind me at the funeral and explaining what on earth was going on," Wanda recalled. "We left Sarah's courtyard and drove, by taxi, to a union hall where the funeral was held. It was the only place available that was large enough to hold a group as large as this." The hall was decorated with an elevated podium, a coffin draped with black silk and a large picture of Sarah, and when the service began, a series of men got up and spoke. But then, the surprise of the day: "The service came to a halt and everything got very quiet and this voice—very low, very deliberate, and a bit weak—started speaking," Wanda wrote. "It almost sounded masculine. Then Hettie Lee Ewing leaned forward and explained . . . that this was a tape that Sarah made two or three months prior to her death."[2]

Even in her last days, Sarah was looking ahead. Those she loved—and the God who loved her—continued to be foremost in her thoughts, taking precedence over personal comfort, fortune, and pain.

"She has done a great work," recalled her longtime friend I. B. Bradley. "This is a work of our Master, and this is a sacrificing and consecrated servant of the Lord."[3]

Inscription from the memorial to Sarah Sheppard Andrews
(as translated by Reiko Nishihara):

Sister Sarah S. Andrews was born on November 26, 1892, as the fourth of nine children born to W. T. Andrews in Dickson, Tennessee, United States of North America. She grew up in Dickson and attended Peabody College. In line with a wish of her mother she set foot in Japan for the first time for the purpose of Christian evangelism on January 16, 1916. At that time she was a young twenty-three years and three months.

On September 16, 1961, at 7:10 PM she died at her home on Tokiwa-cho in Numazu. For more than forty-five years she had loved Japan and the Japanese people, forgetting herself and living as a single person, suffering lifelong illnesses and inconveniences and living frugally on her own resources. She established Churches of Christ in Okitsu, Shizuoka, Shimizu, and Numazu.

Giving all honor and praise to God in line with the 103rd Psalm, she served tirelessly in devotion to the many whom she taught and blessed. We whom she taught tearfully and thankfully pray that we will be able to carry forward our teacher's good work.

NOTES

Chapter 1

1. J. M. McCaleb, *Christ the Light of the World: Ten Lectures Delivered at Foster Street Church of Christ*, Nashville, Tenn., September 5–14, 1910. (Nashville, TN: McQuiddy Printing Company, 1911), 20.

2. Ibid., 21–22; 73.

3. Ibid., 41.

4. Ibid., 58–59.

5. Ibid., 61.

6. Ibid., 63–64.

7. Ibid., 66–67.

8. Ibid., 75.

9. Ibid., 180.

Chapter 2

1. Iki Kashiwagi to Sister Karene Harris, August 13, 1981.

2. http://harpers.org/archive/1892/06/page/0169.html (accessed June 25, 2008); http://harpers.org/archive/1892/10/page/0069.html (accessed June 25, 2008).

3. Erik Larson, *The Devil in the White City* (New York: Vintage Books, 2003), 311; Ibid., 185; Ibid., 181; Ibid., 373.

4. Ibid., 319; Ibid., 15.

5. http://worldconvention.org/country.php?c=JP.html (accessed June 25, 2008).

6. Interview with Elizabeth "Bess" Delk, June 1983.

7. http://www.wscoc.com/history.htm (accessed June 25, 2008).

8. Interview with Bettie Lundy, granddaughter of Will and Adele Andrews, May 2007.

9. http://www.ncset.org/publicaions/viewdesc.asp?id=425 (accessed June 25, 2008).

10. Unpublished recollections of Adele Binga Sheppard Andrews.

11. http://www.dicksoncountychamber.com/community/dickson.htm (accessed June 25, 2008).

12. Interview with Bettie Lundy, granddaughter of Will and Adele Andrews, May 2007.

13. J. M. McCaleb, "A Prospective Missionary." *Missionary Messenger,* February 1915, 3.

Chapter 3

1. Don Carlos Janes, On Foreign Fields, *Word and Work,* August 1915, 17.

2. Don Carlos Janes, On Foreign Fields, *Word and Work,* January 1916, 34.

3. http://www.wscoc.com/history.htm (accessed June 25, 2008).

4. J. M. McCaleb, "Our Debt," *Missionary Messenger,* November 1915, 2.

5. Interview with Bettie Lundy, May 2007.

6. Sarah Andrews, "My Trip to Japan," *Missionary Messenger,* February 1916, 4.

7. Ibid.

8. Ibid.

9. http://www.postalhistorycanada.org/int_pacific.htm (accessed June 26, 2008); http://www.discoverychannel.co.uk/ships/ships_in _detail/empress_of_japan/index.shtml (accessed June 26, 2008); www.langara.bc.ca/creative-arts/publishing/prm/1998/42empres2.htm (accessed June 26, 2008).

10. Sarah Andrews, "My Trip to Japan," *Missionary Messenger,* February 1916, 4.

11. Ibid.

12. Ibid.

13. Sarah Andrews, "Reports and Plans of Work in Japan," *Gospel Advocate,* November 20, 1947, 950; Don Carlos Janes, "Missionary Notes," *Word and Work,* October 1916, 466; Don Carlos Janes, "Missionary Notes," *Word and Work,* August 1917, 356; J. M. McCaleb, "Moving Pictures," *Missionary Messenger,* April 1916, 4.

14. Toyohiko Kagawa, trans. by William Axling, *Christ and Japan* (New York: Friendship Press, 1934), 20, 24, 27, 34, 42–43, 46.

15. Ibid., 47.

16. Ibid., 47.

17. Interview with Elizabeth "Bess" Delk, sister to Sarah Andrews, June 1983.

18. Dr. Minta Sue Berry, "Sarah Andrews: Dickson's Own Ambassador to Japan," *The Dickson Herald,* January 2, 2004, 1A.

19. Interview with Elizabeth "Bess" Delk, sister to Sarah Andrews, June 1983.

20. Kuni Nakajima to Karene Harris, November 28, 1986.

21. Sarah Andrews, "Reports and Plans of Work in Japan," *Gospel Advocate*, November 20, 1947, 950.

22. Ibid.

23. Don Carlos Janes, On Foreign Fields, *Word and Work*, December 1916, 556.

24. Don Carlos Janes, On Foreign Fields, *Word and Work*, June 1920, 180.

25. Don Carlos Janes, On Foreign Fields, *Word and Work*, November 1920, 342.

26. I. B. Bradley, "Sarah Andrews Returning Home," *Gospel Advocate*, February 17, 1927.

Chapter 4

1. Don Carlos Janes, On Foreign Fields, *Word and Work*, March 1921, 86.

2. Ibid.

3. Don Carlos Janes, On Foreign Fields, *Word and Work*, January 1922, 21.

4. Don Carlos Janes, On Foreign Fields, *Word and Work*, February 1923, 55.

5. http://www.karai.com24March2005.http://www.karai.com/archives/2005/03/24/the-modern-epidemic/ (accessed June 26, 2008).

6. http://www.ncbi.nlm.nih.gov/site/entrez?cmd=Retrieve&db=PubMed&list_uids=7564060&dopt=Abstract (accessed June 26, 2008).

7. Don Carlos Janes, On Foreign Fields, *Word and Work*, April 1923, 117.

8. Interview with Elizabeth "Bess" Delk, sister to Sarah Andrews. June 1983.

9. "Catalog Houses Built to Last," *The City Paper*, September 12, 2003, 11.

10. http://www.eas.slu.edu?Earthquake_Center/1923EQ/ (accessed June 26, 2008); Don Carlos Janes, On Foreign Fields, *Word and Work*, November 1923, 341; Don Carlos Janes, On Foreign Fields, *Word and Work*, December 1923, 375.

11. Don Carlos Janes, On Foreign Fields, *Word and Work*, October 1916, 466.

12. Don Carlos Janes, On Foreign Fields, *Word and Work*, May 1924, 153.

13. Don Carlos Janes, On Foreign Fields, *Word and Work*, August 1918, 286.

14. Interview with Bettie Lundy, May 2007.

15. "Sister of Local Man Was Held by Japanese," *The Lakeland (Fla.) Ledger*, September 11, 1946, 4A.

16. Sarah Andrews to friends, December 19, 1953.

17. Toyohiko Kagawa, trans. by William Axling, *Christ and Japan* (New York: Friendship Press, 1934), 73.

18. Ibid., 89.

Chapter 5

1. Don Carlos Janes, On Foreign Fields, *Word and Work*, September 1925, 278.

2. Don Carlos Janes, On Foreign Fields, *Word and Work*, September 1926, 281.

3. Ibid.

4. Don Carlos Janes, On Foreign Fields, *Word and Work*, May 1927, 148.

5. Iki Kashiwagi to Sister Harris, August 13, 1981.

6. Don Carlos Janes, On Foreign Fields, *Word and Work*, April 1931, 118.

7. Don Carlos Janes, On Foreign Fields, *Word and Work*, July 1933, 135.

8. http://www.gold-eagle.com/editorials_05/laborde011305.html (accessed July 17, 2008).

9. Don Carlos Janes, On Foreign Fields, *Word and Work*, July 1933, 135.

10. Ibid.

11. Ibid.

12. Don Carlos Janes, On Foreign Fields, *Word and Work*, September 1933, 171.

13. Sarah Andrews, "Reports and Plans of Work in Japan," *Gospel Advocate*, November 20, 1947, 950.

14. *In Memoriam*, typed pages provided by Bettie Lundy.

15. Don Carlos Janes, On Foreign Fields, *Word and Work*, December 1934, 252.

16. Don Carlos Janes, On Foreign Fields, *Word and Work*, July 1935, 137.

17. R. S. King, "Concerning Sarah Andrews' Work," *Word and Work*, July 1935, 138.

Chapter 6

1. Sarah Andrews, "Sister Andrews Relates Japanese Experiences," *Gospel Advocate*, November 14, 1946, 1076.

2. Don Carlos Janes, On Foreign Fields, *Word and Work*, April 1940, 96.

3. Sarah Andrews, "Sister Andrews Relates Japanese Experiences," *Gospel Advocate*, November 14, 1946, 1076.

4. Ibid.

5. Eiko Kanamaru, "Japanese Baptists' Compromise with Nationalism in 1941," *Baptist History and Heritage,* Winter–Spring 2001. http://findartcles.com/p/articles/mi_m0NXG/is_2001_WntrSpring/ai_94160929/pg_1.htm (accessed June 25, 2008.)

6. Ibid.

7. Ibid.

8. Ibid.

9. "Missionaries and Japan," *Time*, December 15, 1941. http://www.time.com/time/magazine/article/0,9171,772851,00.html (accessed June 25, 2008).

10. Don Carlos Janes, On Foreign Fields, *Word and Work*, August 1942, 224.

11. Sarah Andrews. "Sister Andrews Relates Japanese Experiences," *Gospel Advocate*, November 14, 1946, 1076.

12. http://www.historyguy.com/battle_of_pearl_harbor.html (accessed June 25, 2008).

13. Sarah Andrews, "Sister Andrews Relates Japanese Experiences," *Gospel Advocate*, November 14, 1946, 1076.

Chapter 7

1. Sarah Andrews, "Sister Andrews Relates Japanese Experiences," *Gospel Advocate*, November 14, 1946, 1076.

2. Ibid.

3. Ibid.

4. Ibid.

5. http://www.cis.yale.edu/ynhti/curriculum/units/1982/3/82.03.01.x.html (accessed June 26, 2008).

6. I. B. Bradley, "Sarah Andrews Returning Home," *Gospel Advocate*, February 17, 1927, 159.

7. Sarah Andrews, "Sister Andrews Relates Japanese Experiences," *Gospel Advocate*, November 14, 1946, 1076.

8. Ibid.

9. Ibid.

10. http://www.yoyoue.jpn.org/senseki/sensekie/htm (accessed September 10, 2008).

11. Sarah Andrews, "Sister Andrews Relates Japanese Experiences," *Gospel Advocate*, November 14, 1946, 1076.

12. Ibid.

Chapter 8

1. http://www.oxuscom.com/theology.htm (accessed June 26, 2008).

2. http://www.omf.org/omf/japan/about_japan/christianity_in_japan (accessed June 26, 2008).

3. Ibid.

4. http://www.newadvent.org/cathen/06233b.htm (accessed June 26, 2008).

5. http://www.omf.org/omf/japan/about_japan/christianity_in_japan (accessed June 26, 2008).

6. "Urakami Kuzure Part I," *Chikyu-Shimin Newsletter*, September 1, 2006, 1–2.

7. Ibid.

8. Sarah Andrews, "My Maintenance During the War," *Gospel Advocate*, November 13, 1947, 919.

9. Ibid.

10. Ibid.

Chapter 9

1. Sarah Andrews, "Sister Andrews Relates Japanese Experiences," *Gospel Advocate*, November 14, 1946, 1077.

2. Sarah Andrews, "My Maintenance During the War," *Gospel Advocate*, November 13, 1947, 919.

3. Ibid.

4. Don Carlos Janes, On Foreign Fields, *Word and Work*, January 1944, 24.

5. http://39th.org/39th/aerial/62nd/crew42a.html (accessed July 3, 2008).

6. Sarah Andrews, "Sister Andrews Relates Japanese Experiences," *Gospel Advocate*, November 14, 1946, 1077.

7. Ibid.

8. Ibid.

9. Sarah Andrews, "Sister Andrews Relates Japanese Experiences," *Gospel Advocate*, November 14, 1946, 1077.

10. Ibid.

11. Ibid.

Chapter 10

1. Interview with Bettie Lundy, May 2007.

2. "Sister of Local Man Was Held by Japanese," *The Lakeland (Fla.) Ledger*, September 11, 1946, 4A.

3. Sarah Andrews to Myrtle Thompson, October 29, 1945.

4. Ibid.

5. Ibid.

6. Ibid.

7. Ibid.

8. Ibid.

9. Ibid.

10. Sarah Andrews, "Sister Andrews Relates Japanese Experiences," *Gospel Advocate*, November 14, 1946, 1077.

11. Ibid.

Chapter 11

1. Sarah Andrews to Ada Andrews, November 20, 1945.

2. Ibid.

3. Ibid.

4. Ibid.

5. Ibid.

6. Sarah Andrews, "My Maintenance During the War," *Gospel Advocate*, November 13, 1947, 919.

7. K. Morita. Recommendation. The Shizuoka Prefectural Government. May 1, 1946.

8. Ibid.

9. Sarah Andrews, "Sister Andrews Relates Japanese Experiences," *Gospel Advocate*, November 14, 1946, 1077.

10. Sarah Andrews to J. M. and Elizabeth McCaleb, September 6, 1946.

11. Ibid.

12. Ibid.

13. Ibid.

14. Ibid.

15. http://www.bible101.org/japanmissions/page04.htm (accessed July 15, 2008).

16. Sarah Andrews to J. M. and Elizabeth McCaleb, September 6, 1946.

Chapter 12

1. Sarah Andrews, "My Maintenance During the War," *Gospel Advocate*, November 13, 1947, 919.

2. Sarah Andrews to J. M. and Elizabeth McCaleb, February 20, 1947.

3. J. T. Marlin, "Sarah Andrews Prepares for Return," *Gospel Advocate*, April 29, 1948, 419.

4. Sarah Andrews, "My Maintenance During the War," *Gospel Advocate*, November 13, 1947, 919.

5. Sarah Andrews, "Reports and Plans of Work in Japan," *Gospel Advocate*, November 20, 1947, 950.

6. Ibid.

7. Ibid.

8. Ibid.

9. Ibid.

10. Ibid.

11. Ibid.

12. Ibid.

13. Ibid.

14. J. T. Marlin, "Sarah Andrews Prepares for Return," *Gospel Advocate*, April 29, 1948, 419.

15. Ibid.

16. Ibid.

17. www.usfreeads.com/183256-us.html

Chapter 13

1. Sarah Andrews to J. M. and Elizabeth McCaleb, May 26, 1948.

2. Ibid.

3. Ibid.

4. Sarah Andrews to J. M. and Elizabeth McCaleb, July 15, 1948.

5. Ibid.

6. Sarah Andrews to Elizabeth McCaleb, January 2, 1949.

7. Sarah Andrews to J. M. and Elizabeth McCaleb, May 18, 1949.

8. Ibid.

9. Ibid.

10. Ibid.

11. Ibid.

12. Ibid.

13. Ibid.

Chapter 14

1. Sarah Andrews to J. M. and Elizabeth McCaleb, June 18, 1949.

2. Ibid.

3. Sarah Andrews to J. T. Marlin, February 24, 1949.

4. Sarah Andrews to J. M. and Elizabeth McCaleb, June 18, 1949.

5. Ibid.

6. Sarah Andrews to J. M. and Elizabeth McCaleb, August 5, 1950.

7. Ibid.

8. Ibid.

9. Ibid.

10. Sarah Andrews to friends, December 19, 1953.

11. Ibid.

12. Ibid.

Chapter 15

1. Interview with Harry Robert Fox Jr., July 2007.

2. Ibid.

3. Ibid.

4. Harry Robert Fox Jr. to Bettie Lundy, June 6, 2005.

5. http://www.freepress.org/doit.php?strFunc=display&strID=146&strYear=2004 (accessed July 7, 2008).

6. Sarah Andrews to Harry Robert Fox Jr., June 16, 1954.

7. Sarah Andrews to Harry Robert Fox Jr. and Gerry Fox, December 15, 1954.

8. Sarah Andrews to friends, October 15, 1955.

9. Sarah Andrews to Harry Robert Fox Jr., June 5, 1956.

10. Sarah Andrews to friends, September 6, 1958.

11. Ibid.

12. Ibid.

13. E. W. McMillan, "A Noble Phoebe Has Passed," *Gospel Advocate*, October 19, 1961, 662.

Epilogue

1. Wanda Stuart to Sister Duke, September 21, 1983.

2. Ibid.

3. I. B. Bradley. "Sarah Andrews Returning Home," *Gospel Advocate*, February 17, 1927, 159.